INTRODUCTION

This book is a compilation of what was originally two separate texts. It has been converted into a single volume for the reader's convenience. However, the treatment of history and culture is significantly different and deserves mention here.

The most important difference is stylistic. The tone of the history part is academic, whereas that of the culture part is more expansive, descriptive and anecdotal. A secondary difference is that while both parts contain historical and cultural elements, the emphasis is different. In the history part, cultural material helps to explain political, social and economic events and trends. Historical information is included in the culture part to enhance the reader's *verstehen* of contemporary Korean culture.

Korean history is an extraordinary mixture of events and trends. Against the backdrop of a strong cultural uniformity which started to emerge in the 7th century and has continued up to the present day, we find a pattern of rich contrast. Buddhist pagodas stand side by side with Confucian shrines. The delightful delicacy of celadon procelain and court painting provide a foil to the rough, strong colours, sounds and rhythms of folk painting and music. Periods of enormous commercial growth are set against others of financial decay. Numerous foreign invasions are countered by attempts at territorial expansion. Aristocratic rulers enjoyed luxurious and extravagant lifestyles with revenue gained from poverty stricken peasants. Within the Korean administration, periods of factional strife and political coups contrast with long periods of stability.

The aim of this work is to make sense of the many sides of Korean hisotry, providing a comprehensible introduction to the major events and trends for an educated foreign readership. It assumes no previous knowledge of the subject, yet its introductory nature does not indicate naiveté or simplicity. It provides a basic overview while taking into account the most recent scholarship written in English by historians of Korea.

Concerning historiography, the writer has tried to avoid any description or appraisal of events from a 20th century Western standpoint and has preferred to use language describing change, rather than making tendentious references to progress. Attempts have been made to describe and explain events and trends within their own historical and cultural context. It is hoped that the resulting text will provide some insight into, and feeling for, what it was like to be a participant in the various periods of Korean history.

In partitioning a continuous flow of events into periods, thus imposing the artificial boundaries necessary for ease of exposition, socio-cultural characteristics have been used in preference to any other criteria.

Much of Korean culture resembles that of China and Japan, due to centuries of borrowing from China and exchange with Japan. However, just as the personality and character of the Korean people differ from those of its close neighbours (from China much more than Japan), so the Koreans have put their own unique stamp on borrowed cultural items, making them distinctively their own. In addition, Korea possesses many indigenous cultural features not to be found in either China or Japan.

As a result, Korea boasts many cultural treasures which are worthy of study and appreciation in their own right.

CONTENTS

HISTORY

CULTURE

HISTORY

THE EMERGENCE OF A NATION FROM PRE-HISTORY TO 668

From prehistory to the rise of confederated kingdoms: to AD108

From prehistory to 400BC

Neolithic inhabitants of the Korean peninsula

Although there is evidence that man inhabited the Korean peninsula from at least 30,000, and perhaps 50,000 years ago, it is commonly accepted that these people are not the ancestors of the Korean people of today. That distinction belongs to Neolithic man. In the course of a long historical process, the Neolithic inhabitants merged with one another and, combining with the new ethnic cultures of the peninsula's Bronze Age, eventually came to constitute what we now think of as the Korean people.

It is thought that Neolithic man came to the peninsula in the course of three major stages of migration between 6,000 and 2,000 BC. The basic unit of their society was the clan.

Totemistic in nature, clans gained their identity by association with some object from the natural world. Society was matrilineal and the people practised exogamous marriage with members of other clans. Living by the water, they were hunter-gatherers at first, later developing agricultural techniques. Some economic exchange took place between the clans.

Shamanism

Especially worthy of note is the emergence of shamanism, the central element of the Korean religious mind, in the Neolithic period. A primitive attempt to understand the causal and metaphysical structure of the world, shamanism survives even to the present day in the everyday beliefs and actions of many of the common people. Shamans, the priests of the religion, embody a primitive attempt to control nature by intervening in the postulated causal structure, and their services are enlisted to this day in rural areas.

Shamanism is pantheistic in nature. All natural objects are thought to possess souls whose conscious life is expressed in natural phenomena and all events, whether human or otherwise, are attributed to the actions of the spirits. The sun and other celestial objects are worshipped as beneficent gods and the spirits of great mountains, rivers, trees and stones treated with awe. The symbols of worship are totemistic and include such animals as the deer, tortoise and magpie. Spiders bring bad luck, magpies good.

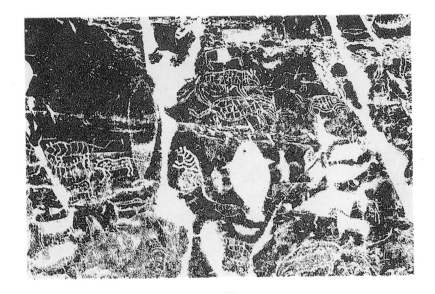

There are both good and bad spirits. The dead possess souls, which travel freely and have a relationship with the living. Deceased ancestors give either blessings or misfortune to living descendants. The house-god controls the happiness or misfortune of the family.

In this world populated by a multitude of gods and spirits, it was natural that some people should rise to prominence as a result of their alleged ability to interact with the spirits; through shamans. The central role of the shaman was to control natural events for man's benefit by exercising control over the spirits.

Shamans functioned as priests, healers and seers. They performed rituals invoking the gods to ensure rain and a good harvest. They performed exorcisms to drive out evil spirits and attempted to foresee the future of the nation as well as that of individuals by divination.

The earliest shamans were tribal rulers, elected for their fighting ability and supernatural power. They could be removed from their position as a result of failing to discharge their religious duties adequately, for example if there was a bad harvest, plague or the clan failed in battle. Gradually, as political structures and duties became more clearly defined, the functions of shaman and ruler separated.

The rise of confederated kingdoms, 400BC-AD108

The Bronze Age

The Korean Bronze Age culture developed around the 8th or 9th century BC and lasted until about the 4th century BC. The people of the Bronze Age occupied the Liao and Sungari river basins and the Korean peninsula. They were slope dwellers with an agricultural society, although they also hunted and fished. Transmitted from China, the cultivation of rice began to be practised at this time.

Possessing superior weapons and greater social organization the Bronze Age people gradually overcame Neolithic man. Society was quite clearly stratified with a wealthy ruling elite who could command the labour service of large numbers of people. In this period, we find the earliest form of state structure in the history of the Korean people, as walled-town states emerged. These were earthen fortifications built on hillside plateaus which controlled the modest agricultural population that farmed the narrow plains which lay beyond them.

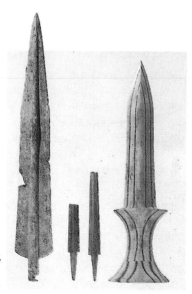

Liaoning-type Bronze Dagger, Stone Arrowheads and Stone Dagger. Bronze Age.

Political developments

Over a period of time, confederated kingdoms, societies with articulated political structures, developed around the walled-town states. By about 400BC, these states had advanced to the point where their existence was known even in China. Of course, the transformation of walled-town states into confederated kingdoms took place at different rates in different cases, and in some instances they never achieved the status of confederated kingdoms.

Ancient Chosŏn established itself in the basins of the Liao and Taedong-gang Rivers. By the beginning of the 4th century BC at the latest, it had combined with other walled-town states to form a large confederation, the head of which came to be designated as king. In the light of assertions by the state of Yen in North China to the effect that Ancient Chosŏn was arrogant and cruel, it may be inferred that it was regarded as a formidable power in the region.

However, by the end of the 4th century BC Ancient Chosŏn began to encounter severe pressure from Yen and entered a period of gradual decline which lasted about a century. During this time it fell successively under the dominion of the Ch'in empire and Han dynasty. As a result, refugee populations migrated eastwards. The end of the kingdom was near and, sometime between 194 and 180BC Wiman, a man of Ancient Chosŏn who had been in the service of Yen, drove King Chun of Ancient Chosŏn from his throne and assumed the kingship.

The subsequent kingdom was called Wiman Chosŏn. Due to frequent contact with the Chinese states, it bore some of the hallmarks of Chinese society, but it was basically a kingdom founded upon Ancient Chosŏn. Wiman Chosŏn was

Bronze shield-shaped implement.
Bronze Age

powerful and ambitious. Pursuing an expansionist policy, it extended its territory northwards, eastwards and southwards to the point where it controlled a region stretching over several hundred miles. Inevitably, such expansion brought it into conflict with the Chinese Han dynasty. Attacked by Han, Wiman Chosŏn fought off the invaders for over a year but eventually fell in 108BC, primarily because of defections and internal dissension.

After having disposed of the threat posed by Wiman Chosŏn, Han promptly established four command posts in and around the Korean peninsula. These were Lo-lang, Chen-fan (later Tai-fang), Lin-t'un and Hsuan-t'u. Chinese control over these areas lasted 400 years, until the command posts began to be pressured by the growing states of Koguryŏ and Paekche. Lo-lang was the principal area in which the Chinese carried out their colonial policy. The Korean people of the area found themselves under fairly benevolent rule as the Chinese allowed political freedom but exercised control in other ways, commanding labour service and transmitting Chinese law. During this period, a great deal of Chinese culture was assimilated by the inhabitants of the peninsula, an on-going event which marked the beginning of many centuries of cultural borrowing from the Chinese. We shall take up the story of the Han Command Posts again in a later section.

The state of Puyŏ emerged in the Sungari river basin in the 4th century BC, and by the 1st century AD it was referred to frequently in documents of the period. By 37BC a splinter group had broken away from Puyŏ to form the state of Koguryŏ in the middle Yalu and T'ung-chia river basins. Developing in the context of conflict with the Chinese, Koguryŏ needed a strong military force and soon came to embody the ethos of a warrior state. Even in peacetime, its warrior aristocracy trained constantly for combat. In order to check Koguryŏ's growth, Puyŏ entered into friendly relations with China and by 49AD an alliance had developed.

The last confederated kingdom of significance is Chin, which occupied the region south of the Han-gang River basin and began to be mentioned in records in the 2nd century BC. Chin was soon restructured into what came to be known as the Samhan (Mahan, Chinhan and Pyŏnhan) when refugees from Ancient Chosŏn flooded into the area and introduced iron culture.

Social structure, culture and social values

Although the confederated kingdoms were, as their name suggests, headed by a king, the authority of the kingship was weak at this time. Real power was exercised by a group of ruling elite and the kings were appointed by election from 2 or 3, or as many as 5 or 6, aristocratic families.

Below this upper stratum were village headmen. Next came the peasants who formed the basis of the economic structure. During the period of the confederated kingdoms, Iron Age culture was introduced to the region, resulting in the construction of better farming tools and increased yield. Mainly farmers and occasionally fishermen, the peasants were not permitted to bear arms. They were taxed heavily by the ruling elite, for whom in addition they were forced to perform labour service. At the bottom of the social structure, there existed a large number of slaves, who had their hair cut short to distinguish them from freemen.

The laws of the period were simple and severe. Further, since it was believed that the gods had ordained that good be upheld and evil punished, law had religious underpinnings and criminal judgements were passed and executions carried out in conjunction with the performance of religious ceremonies.

In all of the Korean confederated kingdoms, the crimes of murder, bodily injury, theft, female adultery and jealousy on the part of a wife were commonly held to be the most serious offences. Known legal provisions may be held to indicate social values. The severe penalties for murder and bodily injury show a regard for individual human life and productivity. Penalties for theft indicate a respect for private property. From the existence of harsh penalties for female adultery and a wife's jealousy, we may infer that attempts were being made to safeguard a patriarchy characterized by polygamy.

As the institution of kingship came into being, the joint functions of religious and political leadership, originally embodied in the single personage of a tribal leader, gradually diverged. Shamanism became more sophisticated and came to occupy a separate role in society from politics.

Bronze Eight-Belled Rattles Bronze Age, 3rd-2nd century B.C.

The rival kingdoms period: (53-668)

A bronze incense burner recently excavated at Nŭngsanri tomb in Puyŏ, the capital of the Paekche Kingdom from 551 to 660

Introduction

In the so-called Three Kingdoms Period, three principal states emerged to partition the Korean peninsula: Koguryŏ, Paekche and Shilla. Minor states, overcome by Shilla in the 6th century, were Pon Kaya and Tae Kaya. Geographically, Koguryŏ controlled the north, Paekche the south-west and Shilla the south-east, with the two Kayas sandwiched between Paekche and Shilla. By the year 53, Koguryŏ had already established itself as a major power in the region, vying with China for control of Manchuria. Next to develop was Paekche, sometime before 246. Last to emerge was Shilla, there being a large confederated kingdom east of the Naktong-gang River by 342.

This period was one in which the three states, each with a rigidly hierarchical social structure and strong military organization, struggled for supremacy in the peninsula.

Social structure: social order, administration and the military

Since Shilla assumed importance (however inaccurately) as the post hoc unifier of Korea, historical attention has, traditionally, focused on the nature of that society to the neglect of Koguryŏ and Paekche. As a result, little of detail is known about the social structure of the latter two kingdoms. However, we do know that all three kingdoms were, essentially, military states with a rigid, hierarchical social structure serving the royal and aristocratic houses. We may, therefore, take Shilla as our example, pointing out differences in Koguryŏ and Paekche as we go.

In this period, the authority of kingship was consolidated as a system of father to son succession developed. Indeed, the entire social order was determined by hereditary bloodline. A man's position in society was fixed at birth and social mobility, beyond certain narrow limits, was impossible.

In Shilla, the system of hereditary bloodline was called the bone rank system (*kol-p'um*). At the top of the system was a core of the aristocracy, which comprised the royal house and those houses from which queens were drawn. Originally, there were two ranks here: hallowed bone rank

(*sŏnggol*) and true bone rank (*chin'gol*). Only those of hallowed bone rank could take the throne. Subsequently, shortly prior to unification by Shilla, the hallowed bone rank ceased to exist, leaving the throne open to those of true bone rank. Following the two grades of bone rank were six grades of head rank, the general aristocracy being comprised of head ranks 6, 5 and 4. At the bottom of the scale were free commoners, presumably comprising head ranks 3, 2 and 1. Thus, a man's status as a citizen was decided. However, the bone rank system did not apply to all men. There were vast numbers of people, the low born (*ch'ŏnmin*) and slaves (criminals and prisoners of war), who were excluded from the system, and hence excluded from participating as real members of society. Even so, one's status as a slave could also be determined by bloodline, as the children of slaves became slaves also.

It is impossible to attach too much importance to the Shilla bone rank system in particular, and the aristocratic system in general. It served not only to establish social position, but also to determine what were acceptable lifestyles and occupations within those positions.

Firstly, various kinds of social and economic restrictions were decided by bone rank: for example, the size of one's residence, the colour of official attire, the nature of the vehicles which one might use, horse trappings and the various utensils which the royal household, general aristocracy and commoners might use. Secondly, one's bone rank determined one's official rank and, consequently, the range and level of government positions which one could hold. For example, in Shilla society there were 17 official ranks. Only those of true bone rank could hold official ranks of 5 or higher, and, since the post of *yong*, the head of a ministry or department, could only be held by someone of official rank 5 or higher, only those of true bone rank could hold it. Hence, we can see that not only did the bone rank system determine one's place in society, it also served as a way of maintaining existing social structures by preventing social mobility. This view is reinforced by the fact that in Koguryŏ, freely contracted marriage between members of different social ranks was unthinkable, due to strict social mores.

In addition to the above system of social segregation, there was a certain status attached to residency in the capital city. People in the countryside were governed by a system of status levels different from those in the capital. For example, there were two grades of village headman, true village headman and secondary village headman, who were chosen from the ranks of commoners and received social privileges corresponding to those received by head ranks 5 and 4 respectively. However, these were *local* government grades, not national, and their holders were denied access to other government positions.

As we might expect, the administrative and military structure of the three kingdoms was also related to the aristocratic system. Major political decisions were made by councils (the *hwabaek* in Shilla, *chŏngsa-am* in Paekche), composed of those of true bone lineage. The capital city was divided into special administrative districts. The countryside was divided into provinces, counties and districts, towns, and villages. The governing position of each was determined by official rank, and hence by bone rank.

Military organization paralleled that of the administration. At the head of the armed forces was the king, who sometimes even led his troops into battle. In each provincial administration, there was a garrison, commanded by the provincial governor. The regular troops were men who lived in the capital, and this elite military force was supplemented in two ways. Firstly, there were oath banner men, part time troops who swore allegiance to their commanders and were kept on retainer. Secondly, in Shilla there was the *hwarang* and in Koguryŏ the *kyŏngdang*, elite corps of aristocratic youth which cultivated an ethos that served the state. In addition, in each of the fortresses that served as centres of district administration, military units of fixed strength were garrisoned, commanded by the "castle lord" who presided over the district.

Taking an overview of the social, administrative and military organization of the three kingdoms, we get a picture of societies based upon power and subjugation. The aristocratic system determined and reinforced a rigid social hierarchy in which commoners, low-born and slaves laboured, with little or no reward, to fill the coffers of an aristocracy permanently prepared for war.

Compared with the overall social system, women of the period fared quite well. In Shilla prior to c.668, women were accepted as full members of society, though without opportunity and recognition in all aspects of society. They possessed sexual equality, they were agricultural workers, they paid taxes, were allowed to head the family and shared equal responsibility with men in supporting the family. In Shilla and Koguryŏ, love marriages were accepted, though such marriages occurred mostly between commoners. Female shamans who functioned as priestesses, healers and seers were allowed to participate in public life and display their ability as professionals.

On the other hand, in all three societies the social position of a woman depended upon the status of her father, husband or son. Kinship rules, customary law and inheritance rules influenced the daily lives of women. In Paekche and Koguryŏ, women were unable to head the family.

Buddhism and Confucianism as instruments of political power

Although the aristocratic system was the basis of society in the three kingdoms, the two belief systems of Buddhism and Confucianism were enlisted by the state as aids in maintaining that structure.

Buddhism came to Koguryŏ in 372, brought by Sondo, a monk from the Early Ch'in, a powerful Tibetan state that briefly reunited north east China. It was immediately adopted as the state religion. A few years later, in 384, the Indian monk Malananta came to Paekche via the East Chin state in the Yangtse river valley, whereupon Paekche also adopted it as the state religion. At about the same time Buddhism made its appearance in Shilla under the leadership of the Koguryŏ monk Ado, but was not popular. It had to wait until a second introduction, c.527 when Wŏnp'yo visited Shilla from the southern Chinese state of Liang, before it was accepted officially.

It is quite clear that Buddhism was adopted officially because it was able to function as a means of state control over the population. Firstly, it was well suited to serve the royal houses. In each of the three kingdoms, society was based upon the idea of a united hierarchy of people serving the monarch. Buddhism, unlike shamanism, reinforced this notion by advocating the notion of a united body of believers all devoted to observing the way of the Buddha. There are numerous examples of Buddhism supporting the state in this fashion. The Sutra of the Benevolent Kings held a high status in the three kingdoms, and "Assemblies for Sutra Recitation by One Hundred Monks" were held to pray for the well-being of the state. Temples were built, dedicated to state protection. Monks exhorted troops to fight bravely in battle, to protect the state, its ruler and Buddha.

Secondly, the aristocracy also found themselves well served by Buddhism. The Buddhist doctrine of reincarnation in a particular life form or particular social position based on *karma* collected in one's previous life, provided an explanation of why people had the social status they did in the strict hierarchy of the societies in the three kingdoms. The commoners, low-born and slaves had the position they did because of their performance in a previous life, so they had exactly the position they deserved. As devout followers of the Buddhist way, they would naturally accept their social position and not envy the aristocracy, who

had presumably performed well in their previous life.

Buddhism served the state in other ways, too. Often, monks functioned as political advisors. In addition they provided ethical guidance to the people as, for example, in Wŏn'gwang's "Five Secular Injunctions" laid down in the early 600's in Shilla: (1) serve the king with loyalty, (2) serve one's parents with filiality, (3) practise fidelity in friendship, (4) never retreat in battle and (5) refrain from wanton killing. Lastly, since many of the people who travelled to China were monks, they served to bring new elements of Chinese culture to the peninsula.

The state maintained strict control over Buddhism, and promoted its spread throughout the kingdoms. For instance, Shilla established abbot administrators at the district, provincial and national levels to control the temples and monks across the whole country. This official version of Buddhism was the Vinaya sect, which emphasized discipline and rules governing monastic life in a unity of belief.

Other forms of Buddhism, although not adopted officially, were tolerated by the state because they were popular with the common people and not in

Gilt Bronze Maitreya Buddha. Early 7th Century.

conflict with state doctrine. One sect held doctrine analogous to later tantric beliefs, maintaining that the power of Buddha could effect miraculous cures, drive off invading armies and slay malevolent dragons. In the later stages of Koguryŏ and Paekche, the Nirvana school became popular, stressing as it did the notion that the imperishable Buddha nature is present in all living beings. It is clear that such forms of

Buddhism could serve as an opiate to a people who might otherwise think that the sole purpose of their existence was to serve an ever demanding aristocracy.

Confucianism also had its part to play in maintaining the three kingdoms' aristocratic social orders, with its emphasis on moral values, the importance of family ties and the notion of the king as the father of the national family.

In Koguryŏ, a National Confucian Academy was founded in 372. In addition, unmarried youths were taught Chinese texts, including the five classics of Confucianism (*The Book of Songs, The Book of History, The Book of Changes, The Book of Rites* and *Spring and Autumn Annals*), Ssu-ma Ch'ien's *Historical Records* and *The History of the Han Dynasty*, and *Literary Selections*. In Paekche, there were also Confucian educational institutions, and Chinese classics, philosophies and histories were read. Shilla came later to Confucianism, but even so, Confucian moral values were widely propagated, as the notion of fidelity could bring society together as one, while loyalty acted as a force directed all the way up the social structure, from commoners to the throne.

The economy and trade

The basis of the economy in this period was agriculture. The staple crop was rice but millet, wheat and barley were also grown. Most, if not all, of the land was owned by the aristocracy, and thus they were able to derive the greatest part of their revenue from rice production in the form of a grain tax on the free commoners. However, other sources of revenue were available. Cloth tax and tribute tax (in the form of goods produced) were exacted upon the peasants. The state was able to commandeer the labour services of the peasants for prescribed periods of time. The slave population carried out the manufacture of many types of good, in addition to grain production and stock raising. These measures, of course, placed a considerable burden on the peasants; so much so that in Koguryŏ, a Relief Loan Law was established. In the spring famine, the peasants could borrow grain from the state storehouse, and repay it after harvest in the autumn.

The principal means of transportation was the ox-cart, although at this time ships began to navigate the inland waterways also. There was even a postal system in Shilla, developed in the 5th century, whereby post was conveyed by horse via a system of post stations. Market places emerged in the capital for local produce. Trade was conducted mainly on a barter basis, although some currency existed, in the form of shells and occasionally Chinese coinage. Foreign trade also existed, mostly in the form of imports from China, although Paekche conducted trade with the Japanese Wa on a limited scale.

Underground storage room to preserve ice for use in the summer months. Demonstration of increased affluence, these were first used in the Unified Shilla period.

The struggle for supremacy among the three kingdoms

Relations between the three kingdoms should be viewed against the backdrop of relations with China and, to a lesser extent, Japan. China consistently pursued policies of expansion. In the face of Chinese aggression, the three kingdoms were forced to protect themselves; sometimes by military action, at other times by forming alliances with the Chinese states, playing one off against the other. On the other hand, it must not be assumed that Koguryŏ, Paekche and Shilla were merely victims of Chinese aggression. They were themselves expansionist and each had its own designs on dominating the others. Moreover, Koguryŏ persistently pursued a policy of aggression towards China, while Paekche attacked and defeated the Tai-fang Command Post. Japan played its role as the longtime and faithful ally of Paekche, often offering its support in times of need.

Against this backdrop, the struggle for supremacy in this period is characterized by a series of shifting alliances and political boundaries, as each of the three kingdoms sought to protect itself and gain power over the other two.

In the first phase of the story, the three kingdoms grew, consolidated their power and expanded to the extent that they began to encroach upon each other's territory. In AD 53, Koguryŏ controlled the T'ung-chia River basin and was pushing south-west and south

(Map 1)

A.D. 53

(Map 2)

53-146. Koguryŏ subjugates Okcho and Eastern Ye.

(Map 3)

244-246. Chinese Wei captures Koguryŏ's capital. Paekche occupies territory of Tai-fang Commandery.

towards the Liao-tung and Lo-lang Command Posts, respectively. By the time Paekche emerged around 244, Koguryŏ controlled the region from the T'ung-chia River basin southwards to the upper Han-gang River. Koguryŏ and Paekche slowly advanced their frontiers, Koguryŏ despite successful attacks against its capital by the Chinese Wei in 244 and Chinese Yen in 342. When the Chinese Chin were driven south by northern nomadic tribes in 316, Koguryŏ was able to assimilate the

newly isolated Puyŏ. By the time Shilla had emerged some time before 342, Koguryŏ controlled the territory of the former Lo-lang Command Post and the north-east of the peninsula to the lower Han. Paekche occupied the region between the Imjin-gang River and P'yŏngyang, bringing it into confrontation with Koguryŏ. Shilla, by far the weakest state at this point, occupied a small region east of the Naktong-gang River. (See Maps 1–5).

By 342, the states had developed and expanded to the extent that they came into conflict with each other. They thus entered into a new phase in their relations and there followed a period of 250 years which was characterized by warfare and shifting alliances, with each other and the Chinese states. Paekche began hostilities, as between 346 and 375 it formed alliances with the Chinese Chin, Japanese Wa and Kaya against Shilla, destroyed the Mahan in 369

(Map 4)

246-313. Koguryŏ defeats Lo-lang Commandery. Renews pressure against Liao-tung Commandery.

(Map 5)

342-371. Chinese Earlier Yen captures Koguryŏ capital. Shilla, Pon Kaya and Tae Kaya have emerged. Paekche destroys Mahan. In 371 Paekche advances as far north as P'yŏngyang

(Map 6)

391-427. Koguryŏ occupies Liao-tung Commandery. Subdues the Sushen in the Northeast, attacks Paekche and extends the frontier to the region between the Imjin and Han-gang Rivers. 427, transfers capital to P'yŏngyang.

(Map 7)

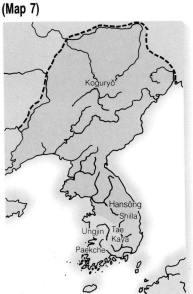

475-532. 475, Koguryŏ seizes Paekche's capital at Hansŏng. Paekche moves capital south to Ung-jin. 532, Shilla subdues Pon Kaya.

(Map 8)

533-551. Paekche moves capital to Sabi. 551, Shilla occupies upper reaches of the Han-gang River. Drives Paekche out of the Lower Han, territory gained during the Shilla-Paekche alliance against Koguryŏ.

(Map 9)

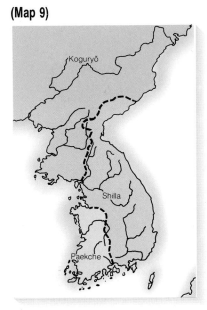

562. Shilla destroys Tae Kaya.

and advanced as far north as P'yŏngyang in 371. In response to the threat against it, Shilla enlisted the aid of Koguryŏ against Paekche in the period 356-402. From 391-427 Koguryŏ took advantage of this alliance and an alliance with the Southern Chinese Dynasty against the Northern, to reach the fullest extent of its expansion. (See Map 6)

This period of Koguryŏ expansion, seeing as it did the capture of Paekche territory, prompted a shift in alliances. In

433 Paekche allied with Shilla in a friendship which was to last until Shilla treachery in 551. During the time of the alliance, Paekche suffered a further loss of territory to Koguryŏ in 475, while Shilla captured the territory of Pon Kaya in 532. (See Map 7)

Then, in 551, Paekche and Shilla launched a counterattack against Koguryŏ, which was suffering internal dissension. The two states pushed northward, Shilla recovering the upper and Paekche the

lower reaches of the Han-gang River. Following that, Shilla treacherously turned against its former ally and seized the territory gained in the lower Han, thus gaining vital access to a port at Namyang (modern Inch'ŏn). (See Map 8)

As a result, Paekche allied with Koguryŏ in 562, the year in which Shilla expanded further by defeating Tae Kaya. (See Map 9) Shilla thus stood alone against a two-pronged attack by Koguryŏ from the north and Paekche from the

(Map 10)

642. Paekche advances as far as the Naktong-gang River.

(Map 11)

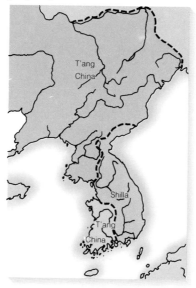

663-668. 663, the T'ang-Shilla alliance defeats Paekche. 668, the alliance defeats Koguryŏ. T'ang establishes Commanderies in the former Koguryŏ and Paekche domains.

(Map 12)

671-713. 671, Shilla expels T'ang from the former Paekche Kingdom. 698, Parhae Kingdom established in the North, under the name of Chin. 713, named Parhae.

west and south.

Shortly afterwards came a time of great trial for the future of the people's occupying the peninsula. This marked a new phase as Koguryŏ played the role of protector of the peninsula against the might of Sui and T'ang. In 589, the Chinese Empire was once again unified under Sui. In order to confront Paekche, Koguryŏ and the Japanese Wa, Shilla allied with Sui, while Koguryŏ formed ties with the newly emerged Turkish power in the north. In 598, Koguryŏ launched an unsuccessful attack against Sui, but then was able to survive massive retaliatory action, culminating in the defeat of a Sui force of over 1,000,000 men in 612.

In 642 there were further developments. Paekche advanced eastwards to the Naktong-gang River. (See Map 10) At the same time schism developed within the Koguryŏ aristocracy with the result that Yŏn Kaesomun, a military strongman, seized absolute power. He openly pursued a stance of aggression towards Shilla, and defied T'ang China by refusing representations that he desist. Consequently, T'ang launched a series of large scale assaults against Koguryŏ, which were resisted but at great cost.

That Koguryŏ managed to withstand successive attacks by Sui and T'ang is a fact important to the survival of the Korean states, but the constant warfare left it much weakened. Its overly aggressive policies, coupled with internal strife, were factors which led to its ultimate destruction.

The final phase of the struggle for supremacy is that in which Shilla emerged victorious over Koguryŏ and Paekche. Shilla prepared carefully for its attempt at conquest. It steadily built up its defences, especially its navy which came to surpass those of Koguryŏ, Paekche and Japan, and enabled it to control the Yellow Sea. Further preparing the ground, Shilla sent a mission to Japan to blunt its military aid to Paekche and allied with T'ang with the intention of crushing Koguryŏ and Paekche. In 660 the Shilla-T'ang alliance defeated Paekche as Shilla attacked by land and T'ang by sea.

At this time, an event of great significance for future events occurred in Koguryŏ. Yŏn Kaesomun died in 665 and a feud developed between his three sons. The ensuing political confusion led to Koguryŏ's downfall. Its grip over the Khitans, Malgals and slaves in the provinces was weakened and subsequent revolts and desertion sorely weakened frontier defences. In addition, two of Yŏn

Kaesomun's sons had little resolve to fight. In consequence of these factors, when Shilla and T'ang attacked in 667, they easily overcame Koguryŏ's defences and Yŏn Kaesomun's sons surrendered their armies, one to Shilla and the other to T'ang. Koguryŏ was completely overcome the following year.

The greatest force in Korea's early history was thus vanquished, and Shilla was left to resist the might of T'ang and emerge as a major state. Once victory was complete, T'ang established command posts in the former Koguryŏ and Paekche domains and began to treat Shilla as a tributary state. (See Map 11) However, in 671 Shilla succeeded in driving T'ang

from the former Paekche kingdom, thus establishing a state whose northern boundaries stretched across the peninsula from the mouth of the Taedong-gang River[1]. Of course, this does not amount to a recovery of all of the territory formerly occupied by the three kingdoms. The result of the struggle between the three kingdoms was the division of land into two further kingdoms, both ruled by people of the Korean race. In 698 the Parhae kingdom, consisting of former Koguryŏ aristocracy and a subject race of Malgal tribesmen, was established in the north under the name of Chin. In 713 it was renamed Parhae. (See Map 12)

Ash-glazed grey stoneware Vessel in the shape of a Shilla Warrior 5th-6th century

[1]. At this point the reader may be tempted to draw parallels between the Shilla "unification" of the three kingdoms and the present problems of unification faced by North and South Korea. He would be advised not to succumb to temptation. The two situations are completely different. At the time of the three kingdoms, there was no sense of national unity and no conscious effort to construct a unified state consisting of one people. Domination was the concern of the three kingdoms.

THE NATION: ITS COMMUNITY AND IDENTITY FROM 668 TO 1700

The Northern and Southern Kingdoms

Parhae: 698-926

Although Parhae ceased to play a part in Korean history after its defeat by the Khitan in 926, it deserves some discussion at this point. By all accounts, it possessed an advanced culture, to the extent that China named it "The flourishing land in the east". At the height of its powers in the reign of King Sŏn (813-830), it occupied vast territory reaching to: the Amur-gang River in the north, the Russian Maritime Territory in the east, the South Hamgyŏng region in the south and K'ai-

yuan in south-central Manchuria to the west. It achieved this territorial expansion despite early conflict with T'ang and Shilla, and by establishing diplomatic ties with the Turks and Japan. Later, it established peaceful relations with China and began, in trading exchanges to an extent extraordinary at the time, to assimilate T'ang culture. It was, then, a major independent state.

However, it possessed an inherent structural weakness, there being a ruling class of émigré Koguryŏ elite and a

subject class of native Malgal tribesmen. Internal conflict arising from this weakness made it easy prey for Khitan attack. After Parhae's defeat by the Khitan, their territory was never completely recovered by the Korean people. Moreover, Parhae's high culture was lost, even though many of its Koguryo elite fled to Koryŏ after its fall. The Malgal tribesmen did not possess the skill required to perpetuate it, while the Koguryŏ elite who fled to Koryŏ played only a minor role in that society.

Shilla: 668-891

Changes and developments in government and society

As the Three Kingdoms period drew to a close, a number of important changes took place in Shilla government and society.

Firstly, following earlier tensions between Shilla and T'ang, peaceful diplomatic relations were established, leaving Korean society and culture to develop unconstrained by the threat of war. Such peaceful foreign relations also provided conditions under which foreign trade could develop. Shilla began to export raw materials to China, followed by hand-crafted articles. There was great demand for Chinese imports, principally luxury fabrics and hand-crafted goods to enhance the already ostentatious lifestyles of the aristocracy. Cultural borrowing took place, as Shilla's aristocracy developed a taste for T'ang learning and fine art, and Korean monks travelled to China to study Buddhism and Confucianism. In addition, there was some economic exchange with Japan and even, to a limited degree, with wandering Arab merchants.

Secondly, important political changes took place as the authority of the throne became stronger, to the detriment of the true-bone aristocracy. For example, Shilla queens began to be taken from a narrow segment of the Kim royal house, further limiting the range of people who might rule. The succession of King Muyŏl (654-661) is also important in this context. Succession to the throne by hallowed bone lineage ended with the two seventh century queens, Sŏndŏk (632-647) and Chindŏk (647-654). After a *struggle* for the kingship a man of *true-bone* lineage, Muyŏl, acceded. This being so it might have been expected that the succession would be somewhat problematic. Even so, Muyŏl was succeeded on the throne by his direct lineal descendants, this fact indicating the heightened authority of the kingship. King Sinmun (681-692) firmly established the authority of the throne by (i) conducting a purge of leading figures at the centre of the aristocratic power structure and (ii) creating political and military institutions which facilitated the use of royal power.

In particular, a new administrative body, the Chancellery Office was created in 651. This was an executive council which was responsible to the dictates of the king, not the aristocracy, and which enjoyed greater status and importance than the *hwabaek*, the aristocratic organ of administrative power.

Military organization also reflected the new power of the throne. Instead of the former six garrisons commanded by true-bone aristocracy and stationed in the provinces, there were nine oath bannerman divisions stationed in the capital and ten garrison units in the countryside, all commanded by the king. The composition of this new national army was important too. Instead of consisting of elite aristocratic troops from the capital, they were formed of men from Koguryŏ and Paekche and Malgal tribesmen, this fact making it easier to exercise command loyalty.

Attempts were also made (in 689) to limit aristocratic power by abolishing the "stipend village" method of salary payment, according to which the aristocracy was entitled to commandeer the labour services of the peasant population as well as gathering grain tax. However, this measure was short-lived as the aristocracy quickly reasserted themselves.

Around the middle of the 9th century, maritime trade began to flourish, reaching volumes far above expectations for the time. Trade with T'ang China and Japan increased enormously, and Shilla's traders came to dominate the shipping lanes of East Asia.

In contrast to the above changes, much of Shilla society continued to develop in the same manner as during the Three Kingdoms period.

The aristocracy continued to accumulate vast wealth. They received grants of tax villages entitling them to the taxes payable by the village peasants, agricultural land to be held in perpetuity, horse farms and grain. Government officials were paid by allocation of stipend villages. The immense wealth gained from these sources of revenue enabled the aristocracy to pursue extravagant lives of pleasure in the capital, Kyŏngju, where thatched roofs ceased to exist, tiled roofs and enclosed courtyards proliferated, and the sound of music and revelry could be heard at every hour of the day and night.

Meanwhile, the plight of the commoners became ever more serious. All faced increased impoverishment. The detailed nature of census documents of the day, which included such items as the number of cattle and horses, kinds of tree and type and area of land, show clearly

A golden crown with gold spangles and comma-shaped jades, 5th-6th century, Shilla Kingdom period.

that the aristocracy made every effort to extract as much as possible from the commoners.

Many commoners were reduced to slavery, unable to repay their debts. In the *New History of T'ang*, it is stated that some of the highest Shilla officials owned as many as 3,000 slaves. If this is so, then the aristocracy as a whole must have owned a substantial part of the entire population.

Both as a salve to the commoners' despair and as a tool for controlling the population by the aristocracy, Buddhism continued to be popular. Monks who had travelled to China brought back with them doctrines of the various Buddhist sects of the T'ang Dynasty: *Nirvana, Vinaya*, Buddha-Nature, *Dharmalaksana* and *Avatamsaka* (*Hwaŏm*, Korean; *Hwa-yen*, Chinese), and Pure Land Buddhism.

The Pure Land sect, which can be traced back as far as the 4th century in China, was disseminated widely among the general populace by the esteemed scholar monk, Wŏnhyo (617-686). Indeed, it is estimated that as a result of his efforts, 90% of the peasant population became followers. According to Pure Land doctrine, one need only to chant "*Nammu Amit'a Pul*" to be reborn in the Western Paradise where the *Amithaba Buddha* dwells. Obviously, such a doctrine would serve to give hope to a population stricken by despair. Pure Land Buddhism was assimilated into Korean Buddhism in a distinctive way. Instead of having the character of a distinct sect as it had in China, it was accepted as a part of the tenets of each Buddhist sect, a development which meshed well with Wǒnhyo's scholarly mission to reconcile differences between the mutually hostile Korean Buddhist sects.

Among the aristocracy, the *Avatamsaka (Hwaǒm)* sect was popular and played a key role, since it preached the all-encompassing harmony of the one-in-many and the many-in-one, a doctrine well-suited to maintaining social order.

During King Hǒndǒk's reign (809-826) *Sǒn* Buddhism (*Ch'an*, Chinese; *Zen*, Japanese) began to become popular. It had originally entered Korea in Queen Sǒndǒk's time (632-647) but at that time it had only been vaguely understood. Its new found popularity as the Nine Mountain Sects of *Sǒn* is due to its becoming the religion of the local gentry. *Sǒn* advocated sudden enlightenment as a result of the spiritual cultivation of the individual mind without the use of texts. This individualistic element in *Sǒn*, coupled with its stress on sudden enlightenment, provided an ideological basis for the local gentry asserting their immediate independence from the centralized authority of the state.

The move towards schism

The trends noted above contain the seeds of destruction for Shilla. The true-bone aristocracy felt themselves to be under attack on two related fronts. Firstly, as has already been mentioned, Muyǒl and Sinmun took steps to increase the authority of the throne at their expense. Secondly, those nobles of head-rank 6 found occasion to ally themselves with the throne against them. Confucianism had a major part to play here. Those of head-rank 6, mostly Confucian scholars, were ex-cluded from holding senior official posts by the bone rank system (see above), while Confucianism emphasized learning and the passing of examinations as the principal criterion for holding office. In addition, head-rank 6 nobles held that Confucianism was better suited than Buddhism to serve as a set of moral standards for human affairs, since Confucianism was social and secular while Buddhism was thought to be individualistic and other-worldly. This, of course, was set against the true-bone strategy of using Buddhism as a means of controlling the people.

Re-enactment of a ceremonial procession of the Shilla period.

Thus threatened, the true-bone aristocracy sought to break the newly acquired authority of the throne. The first signs of unrest appeared during the reign of King Kyŏngdŏk (742-765), only 80 years after unification. This unrest escalated into full-scale rebellion during the reign of the next king, Hyegong (765-780). In 768 a plot against the throne developed, involving large numbers of nobles of the highest official rank and leading to a 3-year conflict. Then, in 774, a high-born member of the aristocracy, Kim Yang-sang, seized power and killed King Hyegong.

From that time, there was no longer a fixed basis for accession, and the true-bone aristocracy developed private armies and formed short-lived coalitions as they strove against each other to seize power by force. There was no possibility of any new monarch establishing stability. He could count for support only upon the private power base that had enabled him to take the throne, and so was quickly toppled by rivals. In the 155-year period from 780-935, no fewer than 19 kings and 1 queen occupied the throne. The strife reached its height in the 26-year period (836-861) during which time 5 kings ruled, including one reign of 18 years.

Obviously, this lack of solidarity among the capital aristocracy left the state much weakened. In particular, it became more difficult to control matters in the countryside. Those of the capital aristocracy who had been forced into the countryside and the indigenous local elite eagerly took advantage of the situation, developing extensive power bases which usurped the authority of the official prefects and magistrates sent from the capital. These "castle lords" used their newly acquired power to exercise economic jurisdiction in villages over which their power extended, levying taxes and exacting labour service on the peasants. Consequently, the government was unable to collect taxes and the economy began to founder.

Finally, in 889, in a desperate attempt to remedy the situation, the government despatched officials to collect taxes. For a peasantry already overburdened by taxes imposed by the castle lords, which in many cases had forced them to become landless wanderers or turn to brigandage, this was the last straw. Enraged, the peasants took to rebellion across the whole country. In some cases the rebel forces were so strong that government forces sent to suppress them were loathe to do battle. In addition to the unending succession of peasant uprisings, a large force of brigands calling themselves the Red Trousered Banditi seized control of the region south-west of the capital. The state was in complete disarray.

These early peasant uprisings did not have the aim of usurping state control. The commoners only wished to improve their miserable lot. Yet as time went on, the situation changed, as two of the rebel leaders emerged at the head of forces strong enough to create new state entities. In 892 Kyŏnhwŏn, of peasant stock, founded the state of Later Paekche, while in 901 Kungye, a Shilla prince thought to have been ousted from the capital, declared the state of Later Koguryŏ (which later became Koryŏ). A despotic and paranoid ruler who justified the execution of those around him by claiming he had a supernatural power to read minds, Kungye was quickly driven from power by his own generals and killed by the mob as he fled. He was succeeded in 918 by Wang Kŏn, the product of a gentry family in the modern Kaesŏng area.

The Later Three Kingdoms and reunification by Koryŏ: 891-935

Detail of inlaid celadon. The crane and clouds symbolize longevity and purity Koryŏ Period.

The struggle for domination in this period was very much two-sided, between Later Paekche and Later Koguryŏ. Shilla, still beset by rebellion and facing the power of the castle lords, completely lost control of the countryside and was largely helpless.

Immediately following his accession, Wang Kŏn (918-943) took measures to strengthen his state. He renamed the state Koryŏ to give the impression he had formed a new state and moved the capital to Kaesŏng, where he had the support of a local power base and could form strong ties with other local gentry. In addition, he established close ties with Shilla, with the intention of destroying Kyŏnhwŏn and securing his position as a successor to Shilla traditions and authority. Such preliminaries over, the hostilities proceeded apace.

In 927, Kyŏnhwŏn attacked Shilla, killing King Kyŏngae. Wang Kŏn took advantage to both attack Later Paekche and be seen as a defender of Shilla. Koryŏ soon gained the advantage, with victories in 930 and 934. Meanwhile, Later Paekche developed internal problems. Kyŏnhwŏn designated his fourth son as his successor. As a result, his eldest son imprisoned him. Managing to escape, he fled to Koryŏ, where he plotted revenge upon his son. In 935 King Kyŏngsun of Shilla tendered formal surrender to Koryŏ. Then in 936 Koryŏ, with Kyŏnhwŏn at the head of the armed forces, defeated Later Paekche and reunification was achieved. In effect, the new state of Koryŏ might be said to have achieved a more complete unification than Shilla two centuries earlier, because when Parhae fell in 926, large numbers of former Koguryŏ aristocracy fled to Koryŏ.

Koryŏ :918-1392

The first phase: 918-1127

The instability of the state

When Wang Kŏn (later called *T'aejo*, Great Progenitor)[2] completed his reunification of the peninsula, he faced a serious breakdown of social order which threatened the well-being of the state. Although his unification had brought to an end the competing regimes, the country as a whole remained in disarray. The castle lords, with their private power bases, still held sway over the countryside and officials could not be despatched from the central government to establish control.

Although serious enough in itself, T'aejo could not even begin to address this problem until he had come to terms with other, more pressing matters. T'aejo himself was a castle lord from a border region who had risen to become king during times of insurrection and disorder. How was he to give himself, and his newly proclaimed state, credibility? In addition, there was the corpus of military commanders of local gentry background who had helped him to victory and who now constituted the new, *de facto*, governing elite. With large bodies of slaves formed from prisoners of war, looted wealth and their own private armies, they were a proud and powerful group. If order was to be established, T'aejo would have to deal with them, either by breaking their power or ensuring their co-operation.

It is natural, given the social conditions of the period, that any attempt to establish the stability of the state in the light of these problems should proceed by trying to strengthen the authority of the throne. The history of the monarchy in Koryŏ, up to the reign of King Mokchong (997-1009) is the story of continued attempts to establish order and the authority of the throne by either limiting the power of the aristocracy or enlisting their support. These measures brought into sharp focus two tensions which characterized the early Koryŏ period: heredity versus merit as a measure of social worth and civil versus military authority. In the end, the tensions could not be resolved, leading to civil disturbance and military rule.

---

2. The founders of dynasties usually inherited the title of *T'aejo*.

Attempts to establish social order: measures and consequences

T'aejo himself made significant progress towards establishing order. Taking a path of least resistance in establishing his credibility, he sought to wear the mantle of authority which had traditionally been Shilla's. In pursuing this goal, he secured ties with the Shilla royal house by marrying a Shilla princess and gained the support of Shilla aristocracy by treating them generously. At the same time, he broke their power by abolishing the bone rank system. He bought the support of the castle lords and the military commanders who had helped him to gain power by establishing marriage ties with more than 20 local gentry families throughout the country, in some cases establishing fictive ties by bestowing the royal surname. With 29 wives who usually resided in the family seat, the marriage was usually consummated when T'aejo happened to be touring the area where the would-be queen resided.

Despite these measures T'aejo remained concerned about his state's stability, and with this in mind, he wrote a series of texts on government, designed to ensure the future well-being of Koryŏ: *Political Precautions, Bureaucratic Precepts and Ten Injunctions*. His fears were well founded, as the next two kings, Hyejong (943-945) and Chŏngjong (945-949) are thought to have been assassinated in a complex treason plot led by a royal in-law, Wang Kyu, who was finally eliminated during Chŏngjong's reign.

In the longer run, his policies had more serious consequences. For one thing, although his policy of establishing marriage ties with local gentry families succeeded in gaining their support, it also opened the door for the aristocracy to amass greater power. Forming marriage ties with powerful families was (and is to this day) a way of improving social and political status, and ties with the royal family were sought after most of all. By judicious use of this strategy, two extremely powerful families emerged which, between them, monopolized political power for about 130 years: the Ansan Kim for over 50 years between 1009 and c.1060, and the Inju Yi for 80 years between c.1046 and 1127. During this period, no less than 10 kings came and went.

For another thing, the abolition of the bone rank system, while serving to limit aristocratic power, created problems of its own. Firstly, all of the many aristocratic houses now held privileged social position and hence were entitled to hold high public office. By what new criterion were officials now to be appointed? Secondly, the entire system of social order was threatened. How was social class in general, and occupation in particular, to be established?

The first problem was addressed seriously during the reign of Kwangjong (949-975), as in 958 an examination system was established. Kwangjong's wish was that people of undistinguished lineage and Chinese with no power base in Koryŏ should receive appointments by passing the examinations. The state was to be governed by a centralized civil bureaucracy, staffed by an elite who were appointed and promoted according to a criterion of merit established by learning, rather than according to heredity. We noted above that in Shilla, Confucianism began to take hold among the head rank 6 aristocracy as a desirable doctrine for government, yet at that time its influence was held in check by the true-bone aristocracy. In Koryŏ, there were no such restrictions on its growth and there emerged a state committed to rule by civil, not military, officials in accordance with Confucian political ideals. Indeed, high military posts came to be filled by civil officials, dealing a significant blow to military power and status.

Confucianism, which favoured a secular approach to the problems of human society, became the orthodox doctrine by which to govern family relationships and the state. Monarchy and aristocracy alike came to regard it as vital to the proper cultivation of political leaders. Yet despite its popularity as a method of government, Confucianism's emphasis on advancement by learning was unacceptable to the new governing elite, the civil and military gentry round the capital. Kwangjong had anticipated opposition from this quarter and, in deference to the strength of the belief in hereditary characteristics as the determinant of social worth, he instituted a protected appointments system whereby one son of a man who reached the fifth rank or above in either the civil or military order could receive a government appointment.

This conciliatory gesture notwithstanding, those high ranking military and civil officials who had been rewarded for their services in founding Koryŏ, not to mention their heirs, were extremely displeased by this measure and stood in opposition to the throne. Despite such opposition Kwangjong stood firm, conducting a bloody purge of all those who stood against him. As a result he managed to assert royal authority over the aristocracy in Kaesŏng.

Kwangjong's hope of appointing figures of undistinguished lineage via the examination system had a limited effect, though, because after his death Confucian scholars of Shilla head-rank 6 background assumed leading political roles. The effect of the examination system was limited in another way, also. In principle, any freeborn person was entitled to sit the exams and hence hold office, but in practice this was impossible. Preparing for the examinations required a great deal of spare time and money, two things which were severely lacking to those of peasant stock. In essence, the examination system represented great social change, but in reality its effectiveness was shackled by

hereditary factors and an aristocracy concerned to protect and further its own interests. On the other hand, its successes must not be ignored. There were many instances of clerks rising to higher office.

The second problem, that of how social class was to be established and how a person's occupation was to be fixed, was dealt with by the creation of a number of occupational orders: the civil official order (*munban*), the military officer order (*muban*), the court functionary order (*namban*) and the soldiering order (*kunban*). Note that the military officer order enjoyed lower status than the civil official order. These orders signified fixed political functions and membership of the groupings was determined on a hereditary basis. It is thought that the unit of inheritance was a family or lineage, rather than an entire clan. It will be evident that the fixing of occupations in a hereditary way provided a convenient way of determining social class, also.

Besides these officially created orders, there were the clerical forces in the local and central bureaucracies and the artisans. Even though they fell outside the officially designated hereditary occupational groupings, in practice these people too were hereditarily fixed in their occupations and social class. At the bottom of the social scale were the peasants, who were ineligible to hold government office, and the lowborn, who were slaves.

It is a striking feature of Koryŏ society that in spite of its structure being largely fixed by heredity, changes in social status took place continually, albeit to a limited degree. As a result of the civil service examinations, there were many instances of local clerks rising to the civil official order. Soldiers could rise through the ranks and enter the military officer order. Further, since depleted armed forces were replenished from the peasant and sometimes slave classes, even they could become soldiers and perhaps rise to become officers and occasionally generals.

Despite such mobility, it must not be thought that Koryŏ was on the way to becoming a liberal society. Its social structure was basically hereditary in principle, and this is the most important point. Instances of social mobility should be seen primarily as by-products of political expediency rather than as expressions of liberalism. They are, however, interesting, since

they worked against heredity and helped people to become aware of merit as a measure of worth, a notion which would assume great importance in the peasant and slave uprisings of the 12th century.

It may be said that T'aejo's attempts to establish order at the beginning of the dynasty generated an interesting interplay between heredity and merit as determinants of occupation and social class, and between the civil and military as holders of ultimate political power.

There were further attempts to establish social stability by limiting aristocratic power. Kwangjong aimed at limiting the power of local gentry and military commanders who had forced prisoners and refugees into slavery by means of his Slave Review Act, which was designed to discover which slaves had originally been commoners and free them.

In 976, during the reign of Kyŏngjong (975-981) a prototypical version of the Stipend Land Law was established, designed to underpin economically the central government bureaucracy which was under construction. This law received far greater definition and force in 998, during the reign of Mokchong. At this time, land

was allocated to officials in 18 stipend grades based upon an office rank structure created under King Sŏngjong in 995. When an official died the land reverted to the state. Further, the collection of land rents was managed by the state and direct collection by officials was not permitted. The Stipend Land Law thus greatly limited the economic power of the aristocracy by limiting the extent to which land could be accumulated on a hereditary basis. It proved impossible to go against the hereditary grain entirely, though, as grants in perpetuity were still made sometimes, in the form of merit land for higher officials who were thus able to perpetuate their privileged positions.

During the reign of Sŏngjong (981-997) steps were made to strengthen the new civil, central bureaucracy. Officials were despatched from the capital to head the local provincial administrative units. The position of the local gentry was downgraded as local government was reformed, and their power was further limited as they were absorbed into the capital aristocracy (largely under royal control) by educating them in the Confucian classics.

The economy and trade

In Koryŏ agriculture continued to be the foundation of the economy and so the distribution of land, along with the peasant workforce required to cultivate it, was of great importance.

The land system had the following basic characteristics. There was public land, owned by the state, and private land, owned by individuals. Public land consisted of stipend land, whose allocation constituted a kind of salary payment to public officials, and public agency land which was used to cover the expenses of government offices. Private land consisted of land held in perpetuity by aristocratic families, privileged merit land, soldiers' land which was allocated to provide a livelihood and cover equipment expenses, and local service land given to local government functionaries.

Within this system and in spite of attempts to limit their power, the aristocracy strove to increase their wealth. Firstly, they increased their private land holdings. As their power grew, thanks to carefully selected marriages, the accumulation of private merit land and the protected appointment system, it

Silver-inlaid
Bronze Kundika.
Koryŏ Dynasty.

became more and more difficult for the state to reclaim stipend land and so more and more stipend land came to be inherited. In addition, the aristocracy forcibly seized the land of others, reclaimed wasteland and sometimes received special grants from the king.

They then used their private land holdings to increase their wealth at the expense of the peasants. They were able to charge a rent of 50% of the harvest on private land, as opposed to the rent of 25% on public land. They then stored their share of the harvest and lent grain at high interest rates.

Wealth became a characteristic of the Buddhism of this

period also, as monasteries increased their land holdings through donations from the royal house and the aristocracy, by commendations from peasants and by seizure. Buddhist land was exempt from taxes, so wealth increased rapidly as the monasteries set up Buddhist endowments, relief granaries and other agencies lending grain at high interest. Further income was generated from commerce, wine-making and raising livestock.

As might be expected, while the aristocracy and the monasteries prospered the peasants underwent increased hardship. As well as having to pay the heavy rent on cultivating private land, they faced a tribute tax, payable in cloth, and adult males aged 16-60 had to perform labour service. The last of these proved especially hard. The peasants had to provide their own food while performing labour service, and there were many instances of poor people working from dawn to dusk without food.

Such hardship forced vast numbers of peasants to flee and adopt a life of wandering or become reduced to slavery. In response to the problem, the government and Buddhist monasteries set up minimal relief programs. These were, however, instituted merely to make profit and conserve the economic base of society and not out of any concern for the peasants' welfare.

Although trade played an insignificant part in the Koryŏ economy, there was a continuation of trade with China, and trade increased with the Jurchen in Manchuria. Export goods included gold and silver utensils, raw copper, ginseng, hemp cloth, paper, inkstones and felt, while imports included tea, lacquer ware, books, dyestuffs and medicines. There was some trade with Japan, and with Arab merchants docking at Kaesŏng's port at Yesŏng.

Everyday life

In Koryŏ society, men were the prominent figures in public life (although upper class women often took significant roles in politics "behind the scenes" as royal consorts, secondary wives or regents.) Women took full responsibility in the family, even to the extent of taking care of family finances. This state of affairs was common to both upper and lower class people, but there were also significant differences in the roles of men and women in different classes.

Among the upper classes, we find that women and men shared almost equal rights of inheritance. Women had little chance to participate in social affairs, but there was considerable freedom for the sexes to mix. Marriage was a means of social climbing and it is thought that at the time of the Mongol invasions the marriage age was about 13. It was customary for the ruler and upper class men to keep several wives. However, there was a clear distinction between first and secondary wives. Secondary wives could be dismissed at will, whereas divorce of the first wife was much more difficult. Divorce proceedings

were, nevertheless, heavily biased against women. Women could not initiate divorce proceedings under any circumstances. Men, on the other hand, could initiate divorce if they had their parents' consent and due reason. "Due reason" was said to be present if the wife was guilty of one of the seven evils propounded by Confucianism: disobeying parents-in-law, bearing no son, committing adultery, jealousy, carrying an hereditary disease, garrulousness and larceny.

Among the lower classes, women were allowed much more social freedom than in the upper classes. They also took on more responsibility for the family. When their husbands were on military or labour service, women provided for their families. A large group of women, probably slaves, took on the role of professional entertainers in song, dance and traditional music. An institute for the training of entertaining women was established during the early Koryŏ period.

The place of Confucianism and Buddhism

The rise of Confucianism as the preferred method of government has already been documented. It should also be noted that the importance of heredity in Koryŏ society led to a modification of aspects of Confucian doctrine. As well as the orthodox procedure of learning in state institutions, there emerged private academies for aristocratic youth headed by former high officials. As a result, a new form of lineage orientation developed, that of one's academic line of descent, or pedigree. In the light of the new developments, the state schools declined, resulting in royal attempts to increase their reputation against the private academies.

It might well be thought that, since Confucianism enjoyed such popularity, the influence of Buddhism was set to decline. In fact, this was not so. Early Koryŏ Confucians regarded Buddhism as a doctrine for achieving spiritual tranquillity and otherworldly salvation that could co-exist comfortably with Confucianism. As a result, many scholars were well versed in both belief systems.

In addition, it was widely thought that Buddhism could influence the fortunes of the state and individuals in this world. It was enlisted by the government as a means of protecting the state and by individuals as a way of realising their own wishes. The building of large numbers of temples, for instance, was carried out in the belief that the many Buddhas would protect the state. T'aejo states this explicitly in the *Ten Injunctions*. Koryŏ also observed a large number of state Buddhist festivals, at which, by means of Buddhist rites combined with indigenous (shamanist) ceremonies, the king and his subjects entreated the various Buddhas and the spirits of heaven and earth to bring tranquillity to the nation and royal house. The publication of the Korean Buddhist *Tripitaka* in the early 11th century was undertaken to protect the state against enemy invasions. Monks engaged in "scripture processions for the fortune of the nation and the blessing of the people, while individuals undertook painstaking pious acts for the realisation of individual wishes.

In this period, Buddhist monks took up arms for a number of reasons. They trained as soldiers so that they could protect their monasteries' growing wealth. They were mobilised by the state in the national defence as, for instance, in the Subdue Demon Corps which was composed to do battle against the Jurchens

Muryangsujŏn at Pusŏksa temple, 13th-14th century.

in the late 11th century. Lastly, they played a part in the political power struggles among the aristocracy.

From a doctrinal point of view, there were significant developments in Koryŏ, thanks to the efforts of the learned monk Uich'ŏn (1055-1101). After returning from studying in China in 1087, Uich'ŏn propagated the *Ch'ŏnt'ae* sect (*T'ient'ai*, Chinese) which contained elements that could be embraced by all of the conflicting *Kyo* (Textual) schools of Buddhism in Koryŏ. *Ch'ŏnt'ae* represented an intellectual effort to reconcile the philosophical study of scriptures with the

method of religious meditation in order to facilitate sudden enlightenment and in addition accorded a prominent place to each of the particular *sutras* which characterized the *Kyo* schools. At first the nine *Sŏn* sects pushed against *Ch'ŏnt'ae* with its continued emphasis on textual study, but later organised themselves under one heading, the *Chogye* sect, which held that while enlightenment could be achieved suddenly without the use of texts, constant study subsequent to an initial enlightenment was necessary. The *Chogye* sect became and remained the dominant Buddhist sect in Korea.

Foreign relations

Foreign relations in this period were characterised by conflict with the Khitans (a tribe of Mongol origin that founded the Liao state) in the north-west, the Jurchen in the north-east, peace with China and a ruggedly expansionist policy on the part of Koryŏ. T'aejo and his successors regarded Koryŏ as the successor to Koguryŏ, and regarded former Koguryŏ lands as their own, to be reclaimed whenever possible, by whatever means possible. As early as T'aejo's time, the northern boundary had been expanded to the Ch'ŏngch'ŏn-gang River.

Koryŏ came into contact with the Khitan after 926, when they overthrew Parhae, resulting in the two states sharing a common border. It is difficult to come to an accurate understanding of the interplay between Koryŏ and the Khitans. It is certain that Koryŏ wished to expand northward, and it is certain that the Khitan were warlike and had expansionist designs of their own, particularly towards Sung China. What is not clear is the part that Koryŏ was to play in the Khitan design.

In 942, the Khitan, in an attempt to establish friendly diplomatic relations with Koryŏ, sent an embassy to present 50 camels to the Koryŏ court. T'aejo, regarding the Khitan as uncivilised and immoral, rejected the peace offering in a hostile manner, banishing the envoys to an island and allowing the camels to starve to death. From the beginning, therefore, Koryŏ adopted a policy of hostility towards the Khitan. Later kings continued T'aejo's expansionist policy. Chŏnjong (945-949) formed the so-called Resplendent Army to prepare for war against the Khitan, and from the time of Kwangjong Koryŏ began to push towards the Yalu River, establishing forts across the Ch'ŏngch'ŏn-gang River. Of additional significance is the fact that the Kingdom of Tingan (Chŏngan), comprised of Parhae survivors friendly towards Koryŏ and hostile towards the Khitan, emerged along the middle reaches of the Yalu.

Under these circumstances, it is hardly surprising that the Khitan began to take action against Koryŏ. The degree of concern felt by the Khitan about the situation may be measured by the fact that in 993 they sent an invasion force against Koryŏ despite their al-

ready being engaged in a struggle against Sung China, their primary target. Unless they felt sorely pressed, they would have been unlikely to expose themselves to attack on two flanks at the same time. Actually, it is not clear how serious their invasion effort was. Combat quickly led to stalemate and a diplomatic resolution was found whereby the Khitan withdrew, granting Koryŏ lands south of the Yalu in return for friendly relations between the two states.

Koryŏ immediately strengthened its position by building a number of fortresses in the area south-east of the Yalu. The Khitan, worried about Koryŏ's swiftly increasing military strength in the area, demanded that Koryŏ return the land occupied by the newly called Six Garrison Settlement. Of course Koryŏ refused, setting the scene for further conflict. In 1010, the Khitan informed Koryŏ that they intended to invade, presumably to give Koryŏ a last chance to return the contested territory and to indicate that they were about to take such action with reluctance. In the absence of a response from Koryŏ, the Khitan army, under Kang Cho, pushed south and occupied the Koryŏ capital at Kaesŏng. The

Koryŏ king, Hyŏnjong, fled south as far as Naju in the south-west corner of the peninsula. Then, having gained half of the peninsula and with Koryŏ at their mercy, the Khitan withdrew. Whether they withdrew from fear that their supply lines would be cut or because they had proved a point to Koryŏ that they were a force to be reckoned with (while wishing to concentrate on their western frontier with China), is not known. It is clear, however, that the withdrawal took place on the sole condition that the Koryŏ king pay homage in person at the Khitan court.

As might be expected, Koryŏ never paid homage and failed to relinquish control of the Six Garrisons. A series of small-scale attacks by the Khitans followed, culminating in a full-scale invasion of 100,000 men in 1018. This time, the Khitan were completely out-manoeuvred. Advancing south to Kaesŏng they encountered a capital well-defended by 200,000 men. They retreated, only to find themselves caught in a pincer movement at Kuju (modern Kusŏng). Their invasion force was utterly crushed, with only a few thousand surviving. Thereafter, neither side wishing to risk annihilation, peaceful relations were established between the two states.

At about the time that peace was worked out with the Khitan, Koryŏ began to be troubled by the Jurchen, initially just a group of tribes which had been under Parhae rule. At first, the Jurchen tribes regarded Koryŏ and the Khitan as suzerain states, with Koryŏ supplying goods and cultural items and welcoming immigrants. However, the situation changed when the Jurchen moved towards unification under the Wan-yen tribe headed by Ukkonae, and began to launch small-scale attacks against Koryŏ. Since the Koryŏ standing army had deteriorated by this time and consisted mostly of infantry, it was usually defeated by Jurchen cavalry. This led to a renewed interest in military organisation under King Sukchong (1095-1105). A special force was constructed consisting of aristocratic cavalry, freeborn infantry and a Subdue Demon Corps of Buddhist monks and in 1107, a massive assault was made under Yun Kwan. The attack was successful and Koryŏ occupied the Hamhŭng plain as far north as Hongwŏn and constructed 9 forts. The success was short-lived, though, as Jurchen counter-attacks,

Koryŏ in the 11th Century

diplomatic appeals, and a jealousy of Yun Kwan in the Koryŏ court led to the return of the occupied territory.

Koryŏ encountered more, and more serious, trouble, from the Jurchen as Ukkonae's younger brother, A-ku-ta, united the tribes and founded the Chin state in 1115. With their strength thus united, the Jurchen overran the Khitan in 1125 and even captured the Sung capital at Kaefeng in 1127. With such successes behind them, they pressured Koryŏ to accept a suzerain-subject relationship with them. General opinion in Koryŏ opposed such a move, but at the

time the rebel Yi Cha-gyŏm (see below) had seized power, and he judged that maintaining peaceful relations with the Jurchen would help him to stay in power, and so he acceded. From that time on, peaceful relations were maintained.

While Koryŏ was struggling with the Khitan and the Jurchen, peaceful relations were maintained with Sung, the only exception being when Sung wished to enlist Koryŏ's aid in attacking the Khitan and Chin from two sides. Koryŏ, unwilling to provoke further aggression, refused Sung's request, which resulted in diplomatic relations being somewhat strained for some time. The situation proved not to be serious, however, and trade carried on as normal.

The second phase: Civil disturbance and military rule, 1122-1258

The 12th century is characterized by disturbances caused by the aristocracy, military revolt and rule, and peasant uprisings.

Civil disturbance

We noted above that the Koryŏ monarchy strove to establish social order by means of marriage ties, the examination system and the Stipend Land Law. These measures were taken within a system based on hereditary social class and occupation. There was ample opportunity for the aristocracy to exploit the situation and increase their power. By means of marriage ties, protected appointments, merit land and land seizure they came to monopolize government posts and greatly expand their land holdings. With the power of some aristocratic families rivalling

that of the throne, the scene was set for insurrection.

Between 1122 and 1170 there were several disturbances, the most significant being perpetrated by Yi Cha-gyŏm, the most prominent figure in the Inju Yi clan, and a monk, Myŏch'ŏng. Yi Chagyŏm had given a daughter as queen to Yejong (1105-1122) and contrived to put Injong, the son of that union, on the throne in 1122. Then, after assuring a monopoly of power by marrying another two of his daughters to Injong, he developed further ambition and attempted to depose Injong and claim the throne for himself. In 1126, Yi's forces managed to imprison Injong and kill many of his supporters, burning the royal palace to the ground. At that time Yi's power seemed unassailable, but it was short-lived, for the following year he was himself attacked and exiled by his opportunistic accomplice, Ch'ŏk Chun-gyŏng, and was never heard of again.

Upon his return to power, Injong considered a series of measures to restore the authority of the throne, but this was a time when the Jurchen were exerting pressure on Koryŏ following Yi Cha-gyŏm's acceptance of a suzerain-subject relationship between the two

powers. At this point a number of gentry from P'yŏngyang, led by the monk Myŏch'ŏng, decided to take advantage of the troubled situation to seize power and create a new dynasty based in P'yŏngyang.

Myŏch'ŏng's plan was to persuade Injong to move the capital to P'yŏngyang, using geomantic arguments to the effect that P'yŏngyang's location was much more propitious than that of Kaesŏng. Then, after having been rewarded for helping to bring about dynastic revival, he would seize power for himself. Injong was sufficiently swayed by geomantic considerations to build a new palace (The Great Flower Palace) near P'yŏngyang, but then Myŏch'ŏng's plan to move the capital met with great resistance from the Kaesŏng burueacracy, not least because in 1134 the new palace was struck no less than 30 times by thunderbolts, an event hardly likely to inspire confidence in P'yŏngyang's topographical propitiousness! Realising that his arguments had failed, Myoch'ŏng resolved to take power by force. He raised an army and proclaimed a new state, Taewi (Great Accomplishment) in 1135, but his forces were defeated the following year.

The rise of the military and the Ch'oe regime

We have already seen that in Koryŏ, military officials endured lower status than in previous times. The civil official order was ranked higher than the military officer order. There was no examination system for the military. Even high military posts came to be occupied by civil officials. Military officials were relegated to lower status economically. The economic and social position of ordinary soldiers deteriorated also, as soldiers' land was either taken away or not assigned, and soldiers were mobilized for labour duty in peacetime.

In addition to these visible grievances, the general attitude towards the military was one of disdain and contempt. Soldiers, and sometimes even commanders, served as mere military escorts. During the reign of the frivolous and pleasure-loving King Ŭijong (1146-1170), 9 soldiers froze to death while serving palace guard duty. Further, civil official Kim Ton-jung used a candle to set fire to the beard of Chŏng Chung-bu, a high-ranking military officer.

As a result of such treatment, seething discontent had charac-terised the military disposition from as early as 1014, when a coup d'etat was attempted. In circumstances like these, revolt was inevitable. The spark that prompted action came in 1170, when Han Noe struck Lt. Gen. Yi So-ŭng in the face. With the battle cry "Death to all who but wear the civil official head-dress" the military, led by Chŏng Chung-bu, Yi So-ŭng and Yi Ko, toppled Ŭijong, placed his younger brother, Myŏngjong, on the throne and massacred countless civil offi-cials. Those officials who es-caped death were not so fortunate later, when in 1173 a plot to restore Ŭijong was dis-covered.

Military rule, which was to last until 1270, was thus estab-lished. The first measure taken by Chŏng and his followers was to replace all civilian offi-cials with military men. State affairs came to be managed by the *Chungbang*, the supreme military council which now be-came the highest organ of government. Beyond establish-ing a monopoly of government posts, however, the newly and self-appointed military officials showed little aptitude for main-taining social order.

Rather, they competed one against the other for wealth and power. They used their posi-tions to expand their private land holdings and take control of the country's economic resources. In their eagerness to compete, they armed family re-tainers and household slaves to create their own private armies. Distrusting each other, the situ-ation quickly arose in which these military strong men en-gaged in constant conflict in their quest for power. In the years 1170-1196 the locus of power shifted almost continual-ly from one strong man to another, until Ch'oe Ch'ung-hŏn and his brother seized power.

The Ch'oe managed to estab-lish, and maintain, order for a period of 60 years, until 1258. The might which they used to underpin order was that of a private army which comprised a basic force of 3,000 men (eventually swelling to 30,000), an elite cavalry patrol (*Mabyŏl-cho*) and the Three Elite Patrols (*Sambyŏlcho*). The last of these originally played a policing and personal protection role, but later took on a com-bat role as a new unit was formed from fighters who had escaped from captivity during the war with the Mongols. This private army was supported economically by the Ch'oe ap-propriation of the Chinju region, from which they enjoyed vast revenue.

During this period of stability, Ch'oe Ch'ung-hŏn brought a clear political policy to Koryŏ government. In a 10-article memorandum presented to the king, he proclaimed his intention to remove supernumary officials, return land illegally seized by the aristocracy to their original peasant owners, reestablish impartial taxation, prohibit the construction of temples (thus attacking Buddhist corruption) and curtail the extravagant lifestyles of aristocratic families. Although it is unclear whether or not Ch'oe succeeded in implementing all of these policies, he certainly cut off political connections between the royal family and the Buddhist establishment, put down the peasant revolts and instituted the reforms mentioned above.

The Ch'oe wielded power in the first place as head of the *Chungbang*, where all governmental policies were decided and administrative directives issued. After 1209, they began to employ civilian officials to deal with clerical matters. During the period of Ch'oe-u (1219-1249), Ch'oe Ch'ung-hŏn's son, the civil officials were organised into the Personnel Authority which handled personnel matters and communications with the royal government.

It is interesting to note that at no time during military rule did the military strongmen attempt to seize the throne for themselves, or threaten the institution of kingship. Ch'oe Ch'ung-hŏn, indeed, wielded complete power over the kingdom, deposing 2 kings and setting 4 more on the throne, but power was wielded over a puppet monarchy without threatening the basic institution.

The peasant and slave liberation movement

From 1172-1202, a large number of uprisings comprised of peasants, slaves and soldiers erupted all over the country. Social unrest had been brewing for some time. From the beginning of the 12th century, there had been a trend towards peasants abandoning their land for a life of wandering, due to the severity of tribute taxes and labour service. Often, these wanderers formed brigand bands, causing disturbances in local areas.

As a result of the military revolt, the situation worsened. In their attempt to develop their own private armies, powerful military families seized land by force and sent private troops to collect arbitrarily set taxes. Living thus in fear and oppression, overburdened by both state and private taxes, it is hardly surprising that the peasants took to the sword.

A series of early revolts, in the period 1172-1193, arose spontaneously all over the country on the part of soldiers, peasants and slaves, against the oppression of local officials. In addition to a plethora of minor uprisings, the major ones were as follows. In 1172, a group consisting mainly of soldiers rebelled in the West Border Region. In 1176, there was a revolt led by Mangi and Mangsoi in the Myŏnghak forced labour camp attached to Kŏngju in the south. In 1182, soldiers and government slaves rebelled in Chŏnju. These revolts were aimed at gaining freedom from unjust treatment. They did not yet consititute a liberation movement.

Later revolts had a greater sense of social ideology. As has been mentioned, the lower classes of Koryŏ had developed a greater sense of social awareness due to increased social mobility. During the period of military rule, this sense was heightened as many *ch'ŏnmin* rose from their lowly status to become petty officials and, in some cases, generals. Peasants and slaves alike began to believe that occupation and social position did not have to be dictated by accidents of birth. As a result, rebel bands began to join together with the explicit aim of achieving liberation. There followed a number of large scale attempts aimed at restructuring the social order and seizing political power, the most striking being that organized by a slave, Manjok, in Kaesŏng in 1198. The plot involved the entire slave population of the capital, and although it was discovered before the rising began properly, it is famous for one of the most stirring speeches in Korean history:

Since the events of 1170 and 1173 many high officials have risen from among the slave class. Are generals and ministers born to these glories? No! For when the time is right anyone at all can hold these offices. Why then should we only work ourselves to the bone and suffer under the whip?.....If each one kills his master and burns the record of his slave status, thus bringing slavery to an end in our country, then each of us will be able to become a minister or general.

Other rebel bands rose against the ruling elite in Kyŏngsang-do province in 1193, 1199, 1200 and 1202. In 1193, the rebel force numbered in the tens of thousands, and it took government troops over a year to suppress it. By the end of 1202, order had been restored, and the slaves had to wait another 700 years, until 1894, for their emancipation. They had, however, succeeded in making a point and, under the direction of the Ch'oe family, their conditions were improved considerably. The special forced labour districts were abolished. Magistrates were posted from the capital to smaller counties which had hitherto lacked such administration. In addition, a tremendous number of *ch'ŏnmin* of all categories were appointed to petty government posts on the basis of ability or services well-rendered. In general, the Ch'oe were conciliatory in dealing with the rebels, often conferring honorary titles and ranks upon insurgent leaders, or promoting rebellious villages or cities to a higher administrative unit as a means of establishing

order. The increased social mobility which resulted from the liberation movement is one of the most conspicuous features of Koryŏ society, but its effect was short-lived, as such mobility became frozen in the Chosŏn dynasty.

Koryŏ and the Mongols in the 13th Century

The third phase: Koryŏ and the Mongols, 1215-1368

War with the Mongols

The Mongols, a tribe of nomadic horsebacked warriors who had their origins in the north-east, were extremely attracted by the wealth of the southern powers of Chin, Sung and Koryŏ. Then, after their defeat of the Chin in 1215 which brought them into contact with the Koryŏ border, they had a further reason to be interested in Koryŏ. The peninsula would serve as a base from which to attack Sung and Japan.

Their first contact with Koryŏ came after 1215, when Mongol attacks pushed the Chin into Koryŏ territory. Koryŏ enlisted the aid of the Mongols in ridding themselves of the Chin, and in 1219, a combined Mongol-Koryŏ force defeated them. This event prompted the beginnings of a rift between the two powers. The Mongols regarded themselves as Koryŏ's saviours, and as a result demanded an annual tribute. Koryŏ often refused to pay, and thus a tension developed. The situation came to a head in 1225, when a Mongol envoy was killed on his return from Koryŏ. The event led to a Mongol invasion in 1231.

Although the Mongols withdrew after Koryŏ sued for peace, they left military governors in north-west Korea and demanded a large gift of tribute, including 1,000 otters and 500 aristocratic virgins. Resolving to resist, Ch'oe-u moved the capital to Kanghwado-Island in 1232, an action designed to exploit the Mongol fear of the sea. While the two sides faced each other in a stalemate across the narrow strip of water, the peasants were left to continue the fight on the mainland, against an onslaught of no less than 6 invasions from 1232-1254. They fought courageously from mountain strongholds and bases on offshore islands, but they suffered terrible losses and hardship. Food was in short supply as the Mongols employed burnt earth tactics, and

the population declined as the defenders were slaughtered and hundreds of thousands of captives taken.[3]

Meanwhile, on Kanghwado, the ruling elite continued their lives of luxury, as grain tax was carried along safe shipping lines. The failure of the government to consider the welfare of the populace led to defeat. The peasants lost their will to fight, creating a crisis in which a sentiment for peace arose on the parts of the king and civil officials. In consequence, the last of the Ch'oe dictators, Ch'oe-ui, was assassinated in 1258. In 1259, the Mongols were approached for peace and finally, after further troubles, the capital was returned to Kaesŏng in 1270.

Even so, resistance by the military men continued, as the

---

3. It was during this period, c.1234, that the first use of movable metal type appeared, in the production of a new edition of the Buddhist *Tripitaka*. Moveable type had been invented by the Chinese in the 11th century, but the type was made of clay and proved unpopular. Thus Korea may take credit for developing the first practical moveable type printing.

Sambyŏlcho established a base on Chindo Island, off the south-west coast, and created a government in opposition. Driven from Chindo in 1271 by a combined Koryŏ-Mongol force, they fled to Chejudo Island, where they suffered final defeat in 1273.

Koryŏ as a son-in-law state to Yuan

At this time, Koryŏ became a son-in-law state to the Mongols, who established the Yuan dynasty in China. Koryŏ kings were forced to take princesses of the Yuan imperial house as consorts, these women having considerable influence in the Koryŏ court. Koryŏ princes had to reside as hostages in Beijing until called to the kingship. Yuan occasionally determined the Koryŏ succession, deposing one king and crowning another. Koryŏ kings took Mongol names, wore their hair Mongol style, wore Mongol clothes and used the Mongol language. As a consequence of these impositions, the institution of kingship was weakened in late Koryŏ. Mongol influence was great, yet despite that, Koryŏ kings did manage to retain their status as monarchs of an indepen-

dent kingdom.

Defeat by the Mongols brought with it numerous other burdens. The peasants suffered enormously as they were responsible for supplying food and constructing warships for the (failed) Mongol invasions of Japan in 1274 and 1281. In addition, they had to shoulder the huge economic levies exacted by the Mongols, in the form of gold, silver, cloth, grain, ginseng, falcons, young women and eunuchs. Finally, Hamgyŏng-do province, in the north-east, was placed under direct Mongol (Yuan) control.

Social change

There were also many changes in society. New powerful families arose due to services rendered to the Mongols in the fields of interpreting, falcon raising and escort. This trend was characterised by a desire for personal aggrandisement. Private landholdings had been growing for some time, but the situation became critical after the downfall of the military, when the increased power of the dominant families enabled them to secure special privileges such as exemptions from tax and labour service.

The growth of the private estates seriously depleted the government's land resources. This led to a decrease in state revenue, which in turn resulted in the government being unable to pay newly appointed officials. In addition, the private estates were cultivated by tenant farmers and slaves, with most of the peasant population choosing to become slaves so as to secure the protection of the land owner. The increase in private slaves led to a decrease in the number of free commoners that could be mobilised for labour service, and so the government had to mobilise the slaves of its own officials. The point had been reached at which the state was unable to ensure the well-being of those for whom it primarily existed, the higher echelons of official bureaucracy.

The rise of Neo-Confucianism and the decline of Buddhism

Towards the end of the Koryŏ period, a new form of Confucianism, initially propounded by the Chinese philosopher Chu-Hsi, began to take hold. This was Neo-Confucianism, an amalgamation of traditional Confucianism, Buddhism and religious Taoism.

Philosophically, it sought to explain the origins of man and the universe in metaphysical terms. Things come into being as a result of the union of two elements, *li*, or form, and *ch'i*, or matter/energy. *Li* is what gives reality its coherence and shape, and contributes what is intrinsically good in it; *ch'i* is what *li* shapes into whatever it is, which includes human beings. The reader should avoid the tempting comparison with Aristotelian thought here. The two are very different.

Politically and ethically, it stressed five fundamental human relationships: monarch and subject with emphasis on the subject's loyalty, father and son with emphasis on the son's filial piety, husband and wife with emphasis on the wife's obedience, elder and younger brother with emphasis on the younger brother's respect, and friendship emphasizing mutual sincerity. The responsibility for proper conduct was placed on the inferior in the relationship in every case, except for that of friendship. Intolerant of any other doctrine, Neo-Confucianism provided a strict code for the government of the state and the conducting of social relationships.

To some, a new class of scholar-bureaucrats who strove for political advancement solely on the basis of examination and not by protected appointment, Neo-Confucianism appeared to be a welcome salve to the moral and political sores of the age. Aristocratic government had disintegrated during military rule, and this new class of civil officials began to assume an important role in government following the fall of the military. They came from the clerical force in central government and the ranks of petty functionaries in local administration. In disposition, they tended to be honest, men of integrity who despised the powerful families who had acquired land by illegal means backed by political power.

As the influence of Neo-Confucianism spread, it engendered an intensifying repudiation of Buddhism. At first, the Neo-Confucians attacked the abuses of the Buddhist establishment which had been growing steadily. Many monks had become corrupt; eating meat, lying with women and marrying. The essentials of Buddhism had become tainted with heretical superstitions derived from geomancy. Temples had become immeasurably rich by profiteering. Priests had begun to take an heretical interest in politics. Criticisms of such abuse were aimed at saving the religion by eradicating corruption. Later, some sectors of the Neo-Confucian group attacked the very institution of Buddhism, holding that its essential doctrines undermined the values of family life and were ruinous to the state. As a result, severe persecution of Buddhism ensued, with numerous temples being closed. There was also a strong reaction against the participation of women in the religion. They were prohibited from visiting temples and becoming nuns.

Although the rise of Neo-Confucianism was to have a radical influence on the structure of Korean society up to the present day, it must not be assumed that it enjoyed a rapid rise to prominence. It is unclear how well the doctrine was understood in Koryŏ and the early part of the Chosŏn dynasty, and it did not achieve the status of orthodoxy in politics and society until the 16th century, about 150 years after the fall of Koryŏ. Neither did Buddhism decline quickly. It enjoyed brief resurgences of royal patronage in the early Chosŏn dynasty.

The Fourth phase: The fall of Koryŏ and the rise of Yi Sŏng-gye

The end of Yuan influence and attempts at reform

From the middle of the 14th century onwards, Yuan began to be driven northwards by the rising Chinese Ming dynasty. A relaxation of Yuan influence over Koryŏ ensued and gave King Kongmin (1351-1374) the opportunity to carry out reforms.

External measures against Yuan were as follows. The Yuan liaison organ, the Eastern Expedition Field Headquarters, was abolished, ending Yuan interference in Koryŏ internal affairs. In 1356, Koryŏ recovered Hamgyŏng-do province. Lastly, Kongmin immediately adopted a pro-Ming stance following the founding of the dynasty in 1368.

Attempts at internal refom, although sweeping in scope and far reaching in intent, were ultimately foiled by the recently emerged powerful families. Firstly, Kongmin abolished the Personnel Authority, which placed constraints on the discretionary exercise of royal authority and impeded the rise of the new scholar-bureaucrats. Next, realising that radical measures were required, he appointed Sin Ton, an obscure monk with no political axe to grind, to carry out a thorough reoganization of government. So briefed, Sin Ton began a campaign against corruption. He dismissed all those of exalted lineage background and appointed men with no connections. He returned land and slaves which had been seized by the powerful families to their original owners, and in many instance set slaves free. Of course, such measures provoked hostility and in the end the powerful families proved too strong, killing first Sin Ton and later Kongmin.

The transition to a new dynasty

The fall of Koryŏ and the founding of the Yi dynasty (commonly called Chosŏn) is inextricably linked with the rise to power of General Yi Sŏng-gye. General Yi did not come from a prominent family of long tradition. He was a military commander from a newly-emerged family of military commanders from the Hamhung area, and he rose to prominence as a result of repeated successes against the raids by Japanese pirates from Tsushima Island which plagued Korea after 1350.[4]

Yi Sŏng-gye's role unfolded in the context of a dispute with Ming. As has been noted, Kongmin had adopted a pro-Ming stance upon the founding of the dynasty. However, in 1388 Ming decided to claim all of Korea's north-eastern territo-

---

4. He was aided in his successes by the first manufacture in Korea of gunpowder by Ch'oe Mu-sŏn, which led to the establishment of a Superintendency for Gunpowder Weapons in 1377.

ry that had constituted the Yuan Ssangsong Command Post. As a result, pro-Ming and anti-Ming factions emerged in the Koryŏ court. The anti-Ming faction, with the king's agreement, took the initiative by mounting an expedition into the Liao-tung region. Yi Sŏng-gye was one of two generals who were second-in-command to Ch'oe-yŏng. Yi was strongly pro-Ming and, against the expedition from the start, he marched his army back from Wihwa Island at the mouth of the Yalu River and conducted a near bloodless *coup d'etat*. The king and Ch'oe-yŏng were ousted and Yi seized military and political power.

Forcing King Kyŏngyang (1389-1392) to abdicate, Yi founded a new dynasty, naming it Chosŏn after the ancient Korean state of Chosŏn. To further indicate a fresh start, he moved the capital to Hansŏng (modern Seoul) after seeking geomantic advice. In order to secure an economic foundation for the new dynasty, he instituted land reform in the form of the Rank Land Law, for details of which see below. This reform was of paramount importance, since it destroyed the economic foundation of the powerful families (thus signifying the end of Koryŏ), and ensured the livelihood of loyal members of the Yi faction.

Chosŏn, the early period: 1392—mid-17th century

Chosŏn's first government and internal conflict

At the beginning of the Chosŏn dynasty, paramount political power was wielded by the Dynastic Foundation Merit Subjects, men of literati background who had been rewarded for their help in elevating T'aejo (Yi Sŏng-gye) to the kingship. T'aejo himself appears to have played a passive role in government. Those literati who held power codified a body of administrative law infused with the Confucian ideals, principles and practices by which the political process of Chosŏn would operate.

To T'aejo's sons and those literati beneath the highest levels, the exercise of power by

Ilwŏlkonryundo, used as the backscreen of the King's chair in the Chosŏn Dynasty.

the Dynastic Foundation Merit Subjects was merely a repetition of Koryŏ's aristocratic rule. In addition, T'aejo appointed Pang-sŏk as his heir, a measure which was extremely unpopular with his fifth son, Pang-wŏn, who had done T'aejo considerable service. There followed a vicious feud between T'aejo's sons. T'aejo abdicated in disgust and two of his sons were killed along with Chŏng To-jŏn, the prime architect of Chosŏn's new governing structure. The result was that Pang-wŏn, as King T'aejong, gained the throne in 1401.

Changes in the administration

From the time of T'aejong's accession through the reigns of Sejong (1418-1450) and Sejo (1455-1468), a new administrative structure was developed which represented a major departure from those of earlier dynasties. Previously, the government had been dominated by a joint deliberative council at the highest level. In Chosŏn, the governing process was directed by the two orders of civil and military officials (*yangban*) who enforced prescribed statutory procedures.

T'aejong changed the Koryŏ Privy Council to a State Council (*Uijŏngbu*) with much diminished authority. He established six ministries, each with the authority to approach the throne directly, which over a period of time led to a decline in the importance of the State Council. Sejong created the Hall of Worthies (*Chiphyŏn-jŏn*), a gathering of scholars who studied the ancient statutes and institutions of China, with a view to reorganising Chosŏn's political structure. Under Sejo the National Code was established, setting in place the administrative structure. In addition to the above mentioned were the offices of the Special Advisors (a legislative and administrative advisory body to the king), the Inspector-General (which surveyed public policy, official conduct and public mores) and the Censor-General (which examined and censured the king's conduct).

The Main Hall of Chongmyo in Seoul, a Shrine dedicated to the deceased Kings and Queens of the Chosŏn Dynasty.

The structure of central government

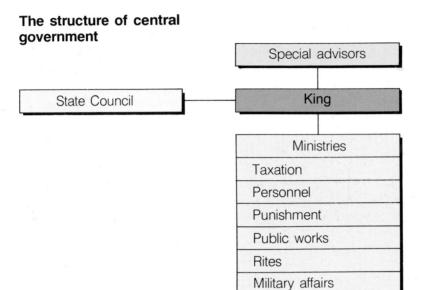

- Special advisors
- Inspector-General
- Censor-General
- State Council
- King
- Ministries
  - Taxation
  - Personnel
  - Punishment
  - Public works
  - Rites
  - Military affairs

In the countryside, there were eight provinces, each presided over by a governor. Each province was divided into counties run by magistrates, whose principal duties were to collect taxes and mobilize labour service. Hence, local government may be said to have served national rather than local interests. The magistrates were assisted in local administration by the county's *yangban* residents who, through the Local Agency, were responsible for rectifying public mores and monitoring the conduct of the county's petty functionaries, the *hyangni*. The *hyangni* performed their duties in the Six Chambers (modelled on the Six Ministries of central government) of each provincial and county administrative unit. Their offices were hereditary, indigenous and unpaid, a combination of characteristics which made venality and exploitation of the peasant population all too easy and common.

Public officials were appointed on the basis of their performance in the civil and military examinations. (A military examination had been set in place at the end of Koryŏ). Now, more than ever before, the official stance was that the administrative structure should be a meritocracy. Although protected appointments still existed, they were offered only to sons of those officials who reached the 2nd rank or above, an extremely small percentage of the bureaucratic corpus. In addition, the policy continued that anyone of freeborn status was legally entitled to sit the examinations and hence gain office. Old habits die hard, however, and we shall see in the next section that as time went on, *yangban* status as a member of officialdom became more and more elitist and hereditary in character.

In the first decades of Chosŏn steps were also taken to strengthen the military, which had been in disarray since late Koryŏ.

Society, 1392-1600ff

The social structure

There were basically four classes of people in Chosŏn society: *yangban, chungin, yangmin* or *sangmin* and *ch'ŏnmin*.

The *yangban*, bureaucrats of the "two orders", civil and military, were the dominant social class and comprised about 10% of the population. They performed only administrative duties and devoted themselves to the study and moral self-cultivation that Confucian doctrine holds is necessary for right government. The civil order was more prestigeful than the military.

As a ruling class the *yangban* were much more broadly based than the aristocratic rulers of earlier periods, hence the increased importance of the examination system. They were, nevertheless, elitist, and gradually became more and more so as they devised strategies for preserving their status and limiting their numbers. They married only themselves, a practice which led to *yangban* status having an hereditary character. They lived in quarters of Seoul separate from the rest of the population and in the countryside inhabited villages, not towns. The descen-

Embroidered front and back section of civil office holders.

dants of *yangban* by secondary wives were prohibited from sitting the examinations. There was regional discrimination concerning higher offices, with most of the high office holders coming from Kyŏngsan-do and Ch'ungch'ŏng-do provinces in the south of Korea.

The extent of the elitism may be exemplified by the fact that anyone who wanted to become a government official had to specify the native place of his family (clan), his date of birth, the names of the four generations of ancestors on his paternal and maternal sides, and the names of his wife's ancestors for four generations. This specification of a man's pedigree was required whenever he was mentioned for a bureaucratic appointment. His

biographical data followed him wherever he went until his death.

As was noted above, in principle, anyone of freeborn status was allowed to sit the examinations. It should now be evident that in practice those of non-*yangban* status were excluded from holding office by those already in power, even if they were fortunate enough to have the time and money to spend preparing for the examinations.

From around 1600, a small class of people emerged directly below the yangban. These were the *chungin* (middle people), petty central and local functionaries including such professional people as medical, scientific and foreign language specialists. It is one of the keys to understanding the period to realize that such specialists were second class citizens. In a Confucian state, administrative duties and right behaviour reign supreme.

Below the *chungin*, forming the bulk of the population, were the *yangmin* ("good people") or *sangmin* (commoners). This class was made up of farmers, craftsmen, fishermen and merchants.

Although most farmers were still tenants, the number of independent peasants, owner-operators who employed hired hands to help cultivate small holdings, rose significantly at this time. This rise in status of some of the farmers notwithstanding, the peasants were kept under strict government control. At all times, they had to display an identification tag (*hop'ae*) which showed the peasant's name, date of birth, class, status and county of residence. In addition, households were organized into groups of five, each of which was responsible for the correct behaviour of the others. These measures were designed to prevent the peasants from abandoning their land and absconding from their area of residence in times of hardship, which in turn was to ensure an adequate supply of labour service and to maintain an adequate level of agricultural production.

The peasants were taxed quite heavily. Land tax was originally set at 1/10 of the harvest under the Rank Land Law. Concerned to improve the peasants' conditions, in 1444, Sejong introduced the Tribute Tax Law, which reduced, the tax to 1/20 of the harvest and had a system for determining the harvest potential of the land. Despite this reduction, the peasants' burden was not eased, for they had to share their harvest with their landlords. 1/3 was the norm, but many paid as much as 2/3. There was also a local tribute tax, levied on products indigenous to a particular locale. Intended to be paid by the local magistrate, in practice it was borne by the peasants. Finally, the peasants had to perform military service on rotation and labour service was required each year.

The status of merchants was particularly low. In keeping with a Confucian disdain for commerce, they were regarded as inferior, greedy and dishonest. They were even, by an act of government, denied the right to use the language of the upper class.

At the bottom of the class structure were the *ch'ŏnmin* (lowborn), slaves and outcasts. Just as in earlier periods there were both public and private slaves. Their status was hereditary and they could be bought and sold at will. The slave population continued to grow during the first three centuries of the Chosŏn dynasty and it is estimated that about one third of the population was legally classed as unfree.

The outcasts were people such as butchers, tanners and wickerworkers. A significant portion of the outcast population were women: *kisaeng* (entertainers), *mudang* (shamans) and healers. *Kisaeng* emerged during the first half of the dynasty and became prominent in the latter half. There were three grades of *kisaeng*: dancers and singers at upper-class functions, singers and dancers functioning as part-time prostitutes, and prostitutes. These women proved to be an extremely popular diversion for men of the Chosŏn dynasty. Many higher grade *kisaeng* became very wealthy, and it was widely held that they were not truly *kisaeng* unless they tried to relieve their patrons completely of their financial resources. *Mudang* were employed by *yangban* and commoners alike for their skill in exorcising evil spirits. They were thus regarded as spiritual healers. Female healers of the

Household items of the Chosŏn Dynasty.

body also played a prominent role in upper-class society, to the extent that a system of training medical women was established as early as 1406.

The class structure of Chosŏn indicated the distribution not only of political power but also of wealth. The *yangban* owned most of the country's wealth, enjoying tax exemptions and other privileges. Merchants and artisans paid business taxes, while the peasants shouldered most of the tax burden. Exploited by landlords and tax collectors alike, and possessing no legal means of escaping from oppression, they often resorted to violence. There were rebellions in various parts of the country in 1467, 1510, 1562 and 1624, while a plot was discovered in 1589.

Everyday life

Everyday life in Chosŏn was governed by the principles laid down by Neo-Confucianism. At the beginning of the dynasty, people's practice deviated considerably from the principles, but as time went on, behaviour conformed more and more to the Confu-cian ideals, ideals which continue to influence behaviour in the late 20th century.

Of considerable importance was the statutory performance of family rites and ceremonies, in accordance with the *Rites and Ceremonies of the Chu Family*, a record of the practices of Chu Hsi's family. Of these rites, the most important were the four ceremonies, marks of new familial and social status: the doing up of one's hair in a new style signifying one's coming of age, the marriage, the funeral and the sacrificial rite for the dead. Every household from the commoner class upwards was required to establish a family shrine for ancestor worship, and there were severe penalties for failing to observe the rites.

The sexes were segregated, with such segregation being particularly severe among *yangban* families. As a rule, women were allowed in the streets only at night and men were restricted to their homes from 9pm to 2am. Women were not allowed to be seen by men who were not close relatives, and consequently they had to veil their faces whenever they went outside. Even within the home, men and women were segregated. Men occupied the outer part and women the inner part of the house, and met only on necessary occasions such as mealtimes. As a result of the segregation, women had little social life and met people outside the immediate family only on special occasions such as the New Year and Full Moon festivals and birthdays. Commoner women were accorded more freedom to move, since out of pure necessity many wives had to work outside the household.

Marriage was allowed only with those outside the blood clan. Penalties for violating this principle were severe and included beheading and hanging. Marriage during the prescribed period of mourning was prohibited and also carried severe penalties. Most marriages were arranged and people could not marry a person of a different social level. The usual age for marriage was about 13 or 14. When married a wife belonged to her husband's family, and widows were forbidden ever to remarry.

Divorce law was similar to that of Koryŏ. A woman could never initiate divorce proceedings, but a man could initiate proceedings if he believed his wife to be guilty of one of the seven evils. On the other hand, we do find a significant difference from Koryŏ concerning the matter of divorce. Even if a

Dagger and tassle worn with the Hanbok, traditional dress of Korean Women. Women used s[...] daggers to pro[...] their virtue.

wife was guilty of one of the seven evils, her husband could not divorce her if any of three further conditions obtained: (i) if she had no-one to depend on if expelled from her husband's household, (ii) if she had borne with her husband the prescribed three-year mourning period for deceased parents or (iii) if her husband had gone from poverty to wealth since marrying.

Women were legally subordinated to men in accordance with the Confucian ethic. Only paternal line relatives were regarded as relatives. Social class and rights were transmitted only from fathers to sons. The sole authority in the family rested with the father, who held control over the children. First-born males held the right

to lineal succession. Women did not have names and were identified only by their position relative to men (so-and-so's daughter, wife or mother). They were forbidden to take part in outdoor games and feasts because it was held that such practices would lead to evil doings. On one day a year, the women of upper-class families used to play a form of see-saw, because that enabled them to leap high enough to see over the walls of the house to which they were usually confined. Mitigating against such overwhelming subordination was a provision that both male and female offspring were legally entitled to inherit the father's property.

The economy and trade to the mid-17th century

The growth of commerce

Sangp'yŏngt'ongbo, late 18th century coinage.

By the 16th century, Korea was enjoying a period of new economic prosperity; so much so that conspicuous consumption and luxurious lifestyles among the upper classes became a social issue. The rise to affluence may be attributed to a combination of factors which emerged during the 14th and 15th centuries: the development of new techniques in agriculture and medicine, the dissemination of new knowledge via the invention of a native Korean script (*hangŭl*), the cultivation of cotton and the expansion of international trade. The most important of these factors were agriculture and medicine.

The first steps towards agricultural innovation occurred in the midst of strategies designed to extricate the Korean people from the miserable situation in which they found themselves following the long period of Mongol interference. Beginning in the 14th century, there was a fundamental alteration in farming practice, consisting in a switch from the traditional fallow field system to continuous cultivation. As a result, the old slash and burn techniques, which required the use of higher ground, fell into disuse and the use of fertilizer on lower ground became prevalent.

The new practice of lowland farming brought with it numerous advantages, which together contributed to an increased yield. The peasants were able to expend less effort going to and from the fields. There was an expansion of available farming land as land was reclaimed from the sea in the southwestern regions and land previously used as horse pasture or military drill ground could be used for farming. Most importantly, there was a gradual increase in the proportion of the wet broadcast (as opposed to the dry broadcast) method of rice planting, which involves the spreading of seeds onto the

main field after it has been flooded with water. The use of this method, which gradually spread from the south to the north of the peninsula, reduced the amount of labour required to weed the fields.

In addition to the change to continuous cultivation, there were other advances in agricultural technology. The wet broadcast method of planting requires good irrigation and the Korean spring, when planting takes place, is very dry. Consequently, systems of dam and waterway irrigation were developed to combat drought. In 1441, a rain gauge was developed, the first of its kind in the world. While it didn't immediately limit the damage caused by drought, information gathered from its use helped to determine the land tax. Better strains of seed were developed and the transplant method of rice planting, which required less labour for weeding than the wet broadcast method, began to be considered (although it did not become popular until much later in the latter part of the 17th century). A gauge to measure wind strength, devices to measure land elevation and distances, and a calendar specific to Chosŏn were also developed. In order to promote the dissemination of the latest developments in agriculture the *Straight Talk on Farming* (*Nongsa chiksŏl*) was compiled in 1430. This important work surveyed farming techniques used in agriculturally advanced regions of Korea.

The government had attempted to promote the advance of agriculture in periods prior to the 14th and 15th centuries, but those earlier attempts had been hindered by a shortage of manpower due to a low rate of population growth, which in turn resulted from a high rate of child mortality. There is evidence that among the upper classes the average number of children surviving to adulthood was fewer than three, and it may be surmised that among the common people two was the norm.

In order to combat this problem, great efforts were made to improve the quality of medical treatment available. From as early as the 11th century, medical research had been conducted, borrowing medical knowledge on paediatrics, obstetrics and gynaecology from China and developing the use of indigenous drugs. By the first half of the 13th century, Korean medical practices had caught up with those of China. By the latter half of the 14th century, the results of the

project began to be seen, as the population began to increase and an annual growth rate of 0.4% was attained. The population of 5,700,000 in 1400 had grown to 10,000,000 by 1511.

It was, of course, important to disseminate knowledge gained to the common people. This was begun in the middle of the 14th century and continued into the 15th. In 1433 the eighty-five volume *Compilation of Native Korean Prescriptions* appeared. This was a survey of all successful techniques of local medicine developed since the newly reprinted *Emergency Remedies of Folk Medicine* was completed in 1236.

These volumes, along with the contemporary *Straight Talk on Farming*, were originally printed in Chinese script. Since the commoners did not possess the learning necessary to understand such script, early attempts to disseminate knowledge were conducted orally by knowledgeable officials dispatched from central government. Conscious of the need for a better way of instructing the general populace Sejong ordered scholars of the Hall of Worthies to develop a native Korean script suitable for representing the sounds of the Korean language. The script,

hangŭl, was invented in 1446. The development of *hangŭl*, easy to learn and easy to read, had a profound effect on the Korean economy as agricultural and medical treatises were reprinted and redistributed. Now even the most lowly peasant could read for himself the latest techniques.

The above mentioned are the main factors contributing to an increase in commerce in the 16th century, when standing markets began to appear all over the country. There had been standing markets previously, but these had disappeared in the chaos of the 13th century. By the 15th century, there were still only a few standing markets, in the capital and provincial administrative centres. The commerce of other areas was handled by travelling markets. However, by the end of the 15th century, as the increased productivity in agriculturally advanced areas began to be felt, new markets opened up and appeared all over the country in the first half of the 16th century. Commerce also flourished in Seoul, as the government opened monopoly shops in silk, cotton cloth, thread, paper goods, ramie cloth and fish products.

The cultivation of cotton and the production of cotton cloth contributed greatly to the development of new markets. Cotton cultivation had begun at the end of the 14th century when an official brought back cotton seeds from China. Cotton cloth was soon in great demand. Warmer than woven hemp yet still reasonably priced, it greatly improved the clothing of the common people. As a result of the great demand cotton cloth became the basic currency in Korea after the mid-15th century, replacing hemp as the medium of exchange. (Coins were produced in this period, but as late as the 15th century were intended primarily for government use in collecting taxes). Demand for cotton cloth was so high that its manufacture became the main household industry, along with making farming tools.

Finally, a link with the expansion of international trade also provided a boost to Korean commerce in the 16th century. Trade had been stagnant even up to the early 15th century due to restrictions on maritime activity imposed by the first Ming emperor, T'ai-tsu (r. 1368-1398). Then, the accession of the emperor Yung-lo (r. 1403-1424) heralded a shift in policy in the form of a drive to export silk and porcelain, with payment in silver. Korean

merchants found themselves in the highly profitable role of middlemen between China and Japan, in the silk and porcelain trade. For its own part, Korea exported grain and cotton cloth to Japan while importing copper, spices and dyestuffs.

The economic boom was not to last, however, and by the latter half of the 16th century had already begun to fade. The causes lay in the behaviour of the Korean upper classes as they pursued extravagant lifestyles and exploited the peasants, in common with the aristocracy of earlier ages.

The distribution of land

The distribution of land, and concomitant inequalities in the distribution of wealth, continued to be a problem in the Chosŏn dynasty. The principles governing the status and allocation of land were as follows. Ownership of all the nation's land *formally* resided in the king, and beyond this, there were two basic categories of land. *Public* land carried with it private ownership rights and was designated as land from which the state

directly collected a rent originally set at 10% of the harvest. *Private* land was distributed to individual rank or office holders with the right to collect the rent. Such land carried with it no ownership rights and reverted to the state upon the recipient's death.

The practice of land allocation deviated considerably from the principle. According to the Rank Land Law instituted by T'aejo, incumbent and former officials were to receive stipendiary allocations of land from the Kyŏnggi region only, according to rank. The rest of the land was designated public land. In principle, land allocations were limited to the lifetime of the recipient but in practice, we find a number of differences from that principle. (i) An official's widow was permitted to retain a portion of her husband's land. (ii) If both parents were deceased "fostering land" could be kept for the upbringing of the children. (iii) Grants of merit land increased. (iv) Most of the land distributed under the Rank Land Law actually belonged to the category of public land, which meant that private ownership rights to it were recognised by the state. In the case of such land there was a crop sharing system between the owner and farmer, whereby the farmer paid 1/3 as a norm, but sometimes as much as 2/3, of the harvest to the owner. For his part, the owner paid a 10% harvest tax to the state. As time went on the crop sharing system spread to rank, merit and other land.

Such practices had two serious consequences. Firstly, there was soon a shortage of land to be allocated to newly appointed office holders. Secondly, yangban landowning and income from the land increased continuously, resulting in the rise of agricultural estates just as during the Koryŏ period under Mongol influence.

As time went on, it became evident that there was to be no workable method of land allocation to office holders. In 1466, because of the shortage of land available to new office holders, Sejo revoked the Rank Land Law and instituted the Office Land Law, according to which allocations of land were authorized only to incumbent office holders. However, this too proved unworkable and was abolished in 1556. Thereafter, office holders were paid salaries.

Threshing rice. Ink, oriental watercolor on paper (Kim Hongdo, 1745-?).

Foreign affairs

Early foreign relations

At the beginning of the dynasty T'aejo adopted a strongly pro-Ming stance, both to confer legitimacy on the new regime and on himself, and to facilitate cultural exchange. He was also in favour of northward expansion and gained control over all of the territory up to the Tumen river frontier, which constitutes the boundaries of present-day Korea. In 1418-1450, under Sejong, these boundaries were made permanent. The Jurchen made two major counter-attacks in 1460 and 1467 but were soundly defeated.

At the opposite end of the peninsula, the Japanese on Tsushima island, being short of food, still made pillaging raids from time to time. Sejong removed this threat in 1419, subduing Tsushima and establishing a peace whereby three Korean ports were opened to the Japanese.

Crisis in the early 17th century

Towards the end of the 16th and in the early 17th centuries, events outside Choson's control occurred which prompted successive invasions by the Japanese and the Manchus. These invasions, coupled with the effects of the little ice age which was making itself felt at the time, had disastrous consequences for Choson.

The Japanese invaded twice; first in 1592 and later in 1597. The view is gaining increased acceptance among historians that the causes of the Japanese invasions lay in the structure of international trade in East Asia. In each of China, Choson and Japan the relative importance of international trade had become so great that it exerted a strong influence on the economic base of the ruling class. The Japanese gradually became more and more dissatisfied with their place in the structure of trade. They suffered from limitations on the volume of trade imposed by China and Choson, and they encountered difficulties with respect to the high commission charged by the middlemen, mainly Portuguese merchants. As a result, they wished to gain control of the original production sites of the goods they imported.

Newly united under the Emperor Hideyoshi and with China as their ultimate goal, the Japanese launched their first invasion in 1592. They quickly advanced from their landing site at Pusan as far as P'yŏngyang, overrunning almost the whole country. Incensed at the Choson government's incompetence and irresponsibility, the general populace refused a call to arms and the country was in a desperate state.

Three factors combined to rescue Choson. Firstly, Admiral Yi Sun-sin inflicted defeat after defeat upon the Japanese navy, using his newly developed "turtle ships".[5] Admiral Yi's naval successes had important effects. The Japanese were unable to move north by sea and supply their land forces, with the consequence that they were compelled to redeploy fighting troops to keep their supply lines open on land. In addition, the grain rich Chŏlla-do province remained in Choson hands. Secondly, the Japanese were harassed constantly as "righteous armies" sprang up all over the country, as the angry peasants resolved to fight to defend their land. Lastly, the Japanese found themselves under attack in the north from a Ming relief force of 50,000 men. Harried on all sides, they steadily retreated all the way to the south-west corner of the peninsula, where they dug themselves in behind

---

5. "Turtle ships" were oval shaped vessels, heavily protected by armour plating and with cannon protruding from all sides.

Chosŏn fleet heading for battle after the Ja

castle-like fortifications.

Peace negotiations began but a solution couldn't be reached and the Japanese launched a second invasion force in 1597. On this occasion, they were beaten on both land and sea, and withdrew in mid-1598 upon the death of Hideyoshi.

The consequences of the six-year struggle were devastating. Many cultural treasures were lost, burned by the Japanese. Korean potters were abducted and sent to Japan, so that the Japanese would not have to import Chinese porcelain. Important books were seized and the learning they contained lost. It is estimated that 100,000 Koreans were taken prisoner and sold to Japanese and Portuguese slave merchants. Famine and disease were epidemic. Land and census registers were destroyed, with the result that the government was hard put to collect taxes and enforce labour service. There were uprisings as the peasants sought to alleviate their suffering.

Before having recovered from the effects of the Japanese invasions, Chosŏn came into conflict with the Manchus. The underlying reason for the Manchu invasions was a desire to expand southwards to gain more farmland. Gradually, the Manchus had ceased to be nomadic and had developed an agricultural lifestyle. Their newly sedentary and politically unified society required increased tax revenue, and the push southwards was designed to acquire an expanded tax base. The situation was exacerbated by the effects of the little ice age on agriculture. As the weather became colder, more and more Manchus made forays southwards in search of food.

However, despite their difficult situation, it seems that the Manchus were not inclined towards territorial expansion until the accession of Hong Taiji (T'ai-tsung, r.1626-1643). Prior to that, there had been conflict with the Chinese (to whom Chosŏn sent relief forces) but the ruler of the time, Nurhaci, did not follow up with a push into China even when Manchu forces crushed those of Ming in 1619. Hong Taiji, on the other hand, held a thoroughly expansionist policy. China was the main target, but the Manchus were also concerned about the threat to their rear posed by Chosŏn, which at the time was ruled by the strongly pro-Ming Injo (1623-1649).

The Manchus found an excuse to invade when, following a failed rebellion in Chosŏn in 1624, the rebel leader Yi Kwal and his followers fled to Manchuria and asked for Manchu aid in righting what they perceived to be political injustice in Chosŏn. Armed thus with a pretext for interference in Chosŏn affairs, the Manchus invaded in 1627 with a small force of 30,000 men. They quickly advanced well to the south of P'yŏngyang, whereupon the Chosŏn government willingly acceded to a demand that Chosŏn would not threaten the Manchu rear during their planned push into China. Having secured this promise the Manchus withdrew.

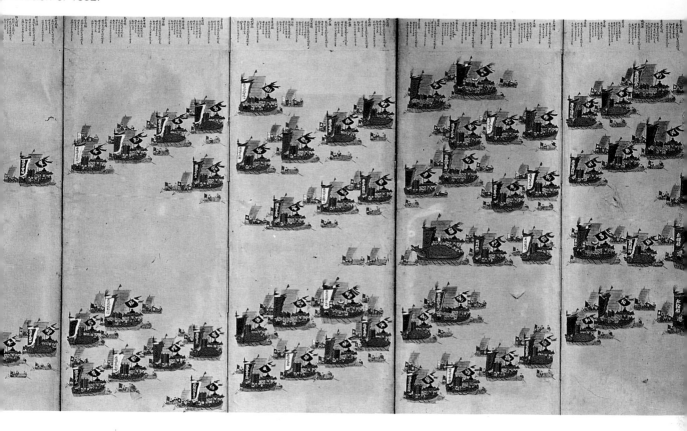

Shortly afterwards the Manchus (who now named themselves Ch'ing), having launched a full-scale invasion of Mongolia, were preparing to advance towards Peking. Still anxious about the threat to their rear, they then demanded that Chosŏn acknowledge Manchu suzerainty. Chosŏn refused to receive the Manchu envoys, thereby reinforcing the northern power's anxiety. With the situation critical, Hong Taiji decided to remove once and for all the threat from Chosŏn and invaded a second time in 1636, with a force of 200,000 men.

The Chosŏn forces were soundly beaten, with several important consequences. Chosŏn was forced to pay homage to Ch'ing as a suzerain power, an event which was to prove of great significance in the 50 years leading up to the Japanese colonial occupation of Korea in 1910. Chosŏn also had to sever all ties with Ming, deliver Injo's two eldest sons as hostages and despatch troops to aid the Manchus in their fight against Ming.

In addition to the specific consequences already noted of the Japanese and Manchu invasions, there were also important consequences of a general nature. During the period 1592 to 1636, the annual rate of population growth plummeted, from 0.4% to between −2.58% and −2.2%. In 1591, the population had been 14,000,000, but by the 1630's, it had dropped to 10,600,000. It was not until 1651 that the annual growth rate reached 0.4% again, and the 1591 population count of 14,000,000 was not reattained until 1679. This severe setback to population growth had a disastrous effect on the economy in the 17th century.

Political strife

The rise of Neo-Confucianism to orthodoxy, 1392-1567

At the beginning of Chosŏn two opposing political forces may be discerned. Dominating society were the so-called "meritorious elite", comprised of Dynastic Foundation Merits Subjects and many others who were later appointed to the status of Merit Subject for services rendered to the state. The practice of appointing Merit Subjects lasted until 1728. These men tended to be opposed to change, pursued policies of personal aggrandisement and were often open to charges of various forms of corruption. Opposed to the meritorious elite and continuing a trend begun at the end of Koryŏ, a new ideological force gradually emerged. These were men committed to Neo-Confucianism and to upholding that doctrine's prescriptions on morality and right government. (However, in mentioning their commitment to purging the government of moral and political impurity, it should not be ignored that such action would benefit their personal careers.) The Neo-Confucians tended to be younger than the meritorious elite,

Yi Hwang (T'oegye, 1501-70), one of Korea's most outstanding philosophers.

having been recently successful in the civil service examinations.

There are two views held by historians of Korea concerning the status of this new group. One is that the younger Neo-Confucian literati, *sarim*, were based in the countryside, thus managing to escape corruption, and managed to enter the central bureaucracy by passing the examinations. They repeatedly attacked the Seoul-based, power-holding, meritorious elite and, despite being crushed in a series of often bloody purges by those in power, succeeded in seizing power for themselves by the last quarter of the 16th

century. The other view attaches no importance to the geographical location of the power base. It posits a single, unitary, socio-political force, Neo-Confucianism, whose followers lived scattered throughout the whole country but whose core lineages lived in Seoul and its environs.

Which view one takes is not particularly important for the purposes of the present work. The central point is that over a period of time beginning in late Koryŏ and lasting until the late 16th century, Neo-Confucianism gradually took hold as the strict and absolute, unquestionable source of political and moral orthodoxy.

As the proponents of Neo-Confucianism secured positions in central government organs, especially the Board of Censors, they were increasingly able to propose policies aimed at the moral reform of government and its officials in the light of Neo-Confucian doctrine. They made themselves the source of endless controversies at court, attacking officials for not only their political views and public conduct but also their private lives.

Their constant and forceful pressure was bound to provoke a reaction. As the high-minded younger officials strove to take advantage of the sacrosanct character of Neo-Confucian dogma to cleanse the government of all impurity (and, incidentally, to rid it of their political opponents), they came under attack from the meritorious elite in a series of four purges in 1498, 1504, 1519 and 1545.

On each occasion, the Neo-Confucians lost the particular political battle they were fighting, but their persistence led to the gradual acceptance of Neo-Confucianism as orthodoxy. By the time King Sŏnjo acceded in 1567, no real disagreement remained on the view that good government must rest upon strict adherence to Neo-Confucian political norms and moral principles. On the other hand, there was concensus that the root causes of the purges lay in the reformists' attempts to apply Neo-Confucian norms too rigidly, and there thus emerged a trend towards a more cautious and responsible exercise of those government bodies concerned with ensuring correct conduct.

Factionalism, 1575ff

The acceptance of Neo-Confucianism as the norm for political and moral conduct did not, by any means, lead to concensus among officials. Desire for personal aggrandisement came to the fore, and the quest for dominant political power led to factional dispute within the confines of Neo-Confucian ideology. Such disputes lasted well into the 19th century and often proved a serious obstruction to political activity.[6]

The general background to the development of factionalism may be described as follows. In Chosŏn, Neo-Confucian doctrine was extremely inflexible and allowed no compromise in its interpretation or application. The monarchy was weak compared with the central organs of

Confucian rite for royal ancestors.

6. It is agreed on all sides that Korean politics of the period was factionalist. Beyond such agreement, there has arisen a controversy among Korean historians concerning the extent to which factionalism obstructed the mechanism of government and whether or not it had a part to play in events leading up to the Japanese occupation in 1910. It would require a large amount of detailed scholarship to arrive at a balanced view of the situation. Consequently, the issue is not pursued here.

administration and so could not prevent internal squabbling. Structural flaws in the design of central government made it easy for conflict to develop and for policy making to be obstructed. Lastly, the rapid increase in the numbers of *yangban* qualifying for office by passing the examinations led to keen competition for posts, which in turn led to infighting.

The immediate cause of factionalism is usually dated at 1575 and is closely linked to the last factor mentioned above. There arose a dispute over appointments to powerful and coveted middle rank positions in the Ministry of Personnel, the office responsible for making new appointments. Obviously, those who controlled the Ministry of Personnel would have a great say in the future structure and views of those staffing the Chosŏn bureaucracy.

As the dispute developed, factionalism was born. The disputants polarised into Eatern and Western factions. At a later date, there were further splits. The Easterners divided into Northern and Southern Men, the Westerners into Old and Young.
The ensuing factional strife possessed clear characteristics which were sure to impede the proper functioning of government. There was a struggle between political cliques, and membership of those cliques ultimately became preordained and permanent. Due to the Neo-Confucian stress on unconditional loyalty, the descendants of those identified with a particular political orientation came to inherit their affiliation generation after generation, so that factional strife became inextricably linked to bloodline. The same loyalty which dictated membership of a faction also operated to stifle individual thought and action, as ''toeing the party line'' was of overriding importance.

The structure of factional strife was reinforced by the master-student relationship in the *sŏwŏn*. These were private Neo-Confucian academies, hundreds of which sprung up from the early 16th century onwards, and which commanded their own rigid systems of loyalty. Hereditary ties and academic loyalties together dictated membership of a faction and hence one's political viewpoints. Loyalties formed in this way transcended all question of right and wrong. In Chosŏn, the inflexibility of Neo-Confucianism served to undermine the moralism which it so strongly advised.

Moralism as a response to crisis

An important aspect of Korean history in the 17th century is that the government consistently dealt with national crises (for example natural disasters and foreign invasions) by discovering their causes in the moral failings of those in power. Such moralism based on Neo-Confucianism had already begun to be noticeable in the 16th century, and the social misbehaviour and political malfeasance generated by the economic prosperity of that time led to an even greater emphasis on a moral critique to counter it. Such appeals to moralism blatantly ignore the role of the natural, causal structure of the world in explaining events and illustrate the blind obedience which Neo-Confucianism commanded among the Chosŏn bureaucrats.

MOVEMENTS FOR CHANGE: MID-17th CENTURY TO 1864

The 17th and 18th centuries

Political development

Following the split of government officials into four factions, membership of which was, as has been explained, hereditary, certain lineages became prominent and began to dominate the process of government. As a result, many Neo-Confucian office holders were excluded from meaningful participation in the political process. In response, many of them retired to the countryside to teach, which in turn resulted in an increase in the number of *sŏwŏn*.

Quite naturally, they also began to criticise the elevation of Neo-Confucianism to the status of unassailable dogma and began to explore alternative systems of thought.

A further consequence of the domination by a single political faction was a weakening of the monarchy and a threat to its continuing power. This situation continued until the accessions of Yŏngjo (1724-1776) and his successor Chŏngjo (1776-1800). These two monarchs were strong and

ruled with true authority. In an attempt to put an end to factional disputes they adopted a system of impartiality, whereby men of all factional affiliations were to be appointed in equal favour, without regard to their affiliation. In the short term, this policy led to greater stability in government and a respite in factional strife. In the long term, it treated only the symptoms, not the root causes, of factionalism, and following the death of Chŏngjo disputes began anew.

Changes in the tax structure

From 1600 onwards, Chosŏn faced a dismal fiscal situation. Farmland had been laid waste in the wars, with the result that the area under cultivation had decreased. Many land registers had been destroyed and the number of "hidden fields", those kept off the government registers by those in power, had increased. Hence, government revenues from land tax had dropped alarmingly and there was a pressing need to find new ways of generating income for the state.

As a result, the Tribute Tax system was abolished and the Uniform Land Tax established in 1608. According to the new law, the land tax would be set at a mere 1% of the harvest. At first, the law was enforced only in Kyŏnggi-do province and in 1623 was extended to Kangwŏn-do province. It could not be extended further at that time, because of the Manchu invasions. It began to be enforced more widely in the 1650's and covered the whole country in 1708. As we shall see, the abolition of the Tribute Tax proved to have a beneficial effect on the economy as a whole.

Since the revenue from the new land tax was set at only 1% of the harvest, alternative sources had to be found. The government therefore instituted a Military Cloth Tax to support the Military Training Command which had been established during the Japanese invasions. The required payment was extremely heavy; two bolts of cotton cloth per year. The Military Cloth tax was the principal source of government revenue, but it placed too heavy a burden on the peasants. Many of them fled to escape the burden, and unpaid taxes were collected forcibly from their neighbours or kinsmen. Eventually, in 1750, Yŏngjo reduced the payment to one bolt of cotton cloth and proposed that the loss in revenue be made up by a variety of minor levies, including a grain surtax. This measure was called the Equalized Tax Law. Its administration was much abused by officials, but there is evidence that it did help to counteract the flight of impoverished peasants.

Party by the Lotus Pond by Shin Yun-bok (1758-?) depicting Yangban society at that time. Ink and oriental Watercolor on Paper.

Revival of the economy

*As Chosŏn gradually reco-
vered from the disasters of the
early 17th century and the
population attained its former
levels, the economy began to
recover.*

Agriculture

In the late 17th century,
because of the sharp drop
in population, there was a
keenly felt need to reduce the
amount of agricultural labour
required to cultivate a fixed
portion of land. Consequently,
the government promoted the
dissemination of the transplanta-
tion method of rice cultivation.
This had two major benefits.
Firstly, the amount of labour
was reduced with the result that
more land could be cultivated
by the same workforce. This
engendered "enlarged scale
farming" as some farmers used
their new found labour power
to cultivate additional land.
Those who practised enlarged
scale farming became small
agricultural entrepreneurs,
producing for the market as
well as for their own consumption. Secondly, a system of
double cropping began. When
the transplanting method is
used, the rice seedlings are

originally grown in seedbeds
and then placed in the fields.
This meant that while the rice
seedlings were growing the
fields could be used for the
ripening winter barley crop.

A further development in
agriculture was the change
from share cost to simple fee
farming. According to the
older, share cost system, the
farmer shared the harvest with
his landlord, and the landlord
bore the production costs and
risk. The landlord retained control of how to use the land. On
the simple fee system, the
tenant farmer payed a fixed fee
to the landlord for the use of
the land, agreeing to bear the
production costs and risk himself. Free of the landlord's su-
pervision, the farmer could use
the land as he thought best,
which led to increased productivity and increased wealth for
some farmers. The simple fee
system became more and more
prevalent as time went on.

International trade

International trade also
provided a boost to the
economy in this period.
From the mid-17th century on-

wards, intermediary trade between China and Japan
resumed following the reopen-
ing of diplomatic relations between Korea and Japan in
1609. Korean merchants made
great profits as middlemen in
the trade of raw and processed
silk that passed through the
warehouses of the newly reo-
pened Japanese mission in
Korea. The volume of exports
of raw silk to Japan at the end
of the 17th century comprised
60%-70% of the total Korean
exports, and the profit margin
was at least 300%.

However, the boom in the
silk trade was to be relatively
shortlived. In 1684 Ch'ing China and Tokugawa Japan established relations, and by the
1720's the volume of trade
passing through Korea began to
decline as China sold raw silk
to Japan directly. Yet despite
that, Korea's overall export
drive did not suffer. The
Korean merchants began to develop ginseng (*insam*) as a new
export item. It was extremely
popular, and to this day is as
popular as silk. To fuel the export drive there was an increased cultivation of ginseng,
especially in the Kaesŏng area.
In order to increase international trade still further, tobacco
and cotton cloth were also cultivated.

Commerce

The 17th and 18th centuries saw great change in commercial activity, as a middle class of merchants emerged.

Firstly, the abolition of the Tribute Tax had the indirect consequence of benefiting commerce. The government did not, of course, lose its desire for the goods once collected as tribute. As an alternative measure, it designated special merchants called tribute men (*kongin*) to serve as purchasing agents for required goods, and independent artisans emerged who produced goods on demand for them.

Although they continued to act as agents for the government, the overall economic activities of the tribute men were far broader. They also did business with the government monopolies in Seoul, inland market and coastal trade brokers and dealt directly with the craftsmen who produced desired goods. They thus constituted a specialized class of wholesale merchants.

Private merchants also thrived, becoming prominent throughout the country. They dealt principally in the grain, salt and fish trades and boat

A hat, backpack and straw sandals used by "Pobusan, a peddler of the la Chosŏn period.

building. In addition, once the licenses to government monopolies were largely withdrawn in 1791, they opened three great markets in Seoul, two of which survive to the present day: Tongdaemun, Namdaemun and one in the Chongno area. As a result of the increase in commercial activity, in the 18th century there arose markets in over a thousand locations all over the country, the large ones being permanent. Their activities included wholesaling, warehousing, consignment selling, transportation, innkeeping, and banking and finance.

One further development worthy of note is the emergence of artisans and craftsmen as private labourers. In all periods prior to this, such workers had been under government control, but in the 18th century they managed to break free. At that time the large majority of them were unable to finance business operations with their own capital and functioned as wage labourers to merchants. Some of them, on the other hand, did manage to start their own businesses as owner-operators and this trend continued as time progressed.

The increased volume of commerce engendered a change in the medium of exchange, as coinage gradually replaced cloth. Copper coins began to be minted in 1678 and by the end of the 17th century were in use throughout the country. Marketing transactions, payment of wages and payment of taxes by coin all gradually became more common, and eventually even land rents came to be paid in the new currency.

Social change

Due to developments in agriculture and the increased commercial activity, society underwent great change. Gradually, a mercantile middle class arose, and in general status lines became blurred as social mobility, both upward and downward, became more common.

Firstly, the changes in the tax structure increased the burden on the peasants and resulted in many peasants becoming poverty stricken and abandoning their land. (i) As was stated above, the Military Cloth Tax proved especially heavy. (ii) Even though the Tribute Tax was abolished officially, the government continued to collect tribute from the peasants when they required it. (iii) Though the Equalized Tax Law did help in some small degree to prevent the peasants' flight from their lands, it really did not alleviate their suffering very much. It was subject to abuse by officials, so that in practice the villagers had to pay more than the legal one bolt of cloth. Also, one burden was simply replaced by another, as the peasants were required to pay a rice tax to compensate for the reduction in the cloth tax.

Secondly, while the lot of some peasants worsened, that of others improved dramatically as they improved their status and increased their wealth by means of enlarged scale farming.

Thirdly, similar developments occurred in the ranks of the merchants. The wholesale merchants rose in status and became rich, while many small merchants faced ruin.

Finally, increasing numbers of descendants of *yangban* lineages were unable to maintain their former lifestyles, and were sinking to the status of peasant, and even tenant farmers.

Increased urbanisation was also a trend of the period, as those peasants who suffered most from natural disasters and tax burdens fled to Seoul and provincial urban centres in search of relief and employment. One consequence of the increased urban population was the replacement of enforced labour service by a "stand-in" labour service, whereby peasants were hired to serve the compulsory labour service of others.

Korean traditional Houses with tiled roofs.

The beginnings of Western influence

In the early 17th century, we find the first appearance of Western culture and scholarship in Korea as travellers to China brought back examples: calendars, alarm clocks, muskets, telescopes, maps of Europe, Catholic texts and texts on astronomy. However, the knowledge represented by such examples was fragmentary and generated little interest at the time, especially during the period of foreign invasions.

In the late 17th century, people began to take much greater interest in the new ideas and technology and there was an advance in understanding. In particular, Korean scholars mastered the principles underlying Western calendrical theory and there was wide acceptance of the principles surrounding the thesis that the earth is round.

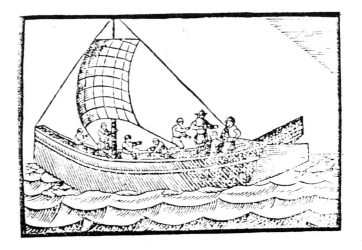

Two illustrations from the Dutchman Hendrik Hamel's description du Royaume de Coree, Amsterdam, 1668: the one above is of his boat drifting and the other depicts his landing on Chejudo Island. Hamel was one of the first Europeans to visit Korea.

Responses to change

It should be evident from earlier sections that the period from the mid-17th century to the late 18th century was one of great change. Such change engendered a number of responses among those who governed, especially the Neo-Confucian literati who had retired to the countryside following the domination of government by the lineages of one political faction.

In response to political developments, there was criticism of the elevation of Neo-Confucianism to the position of unassailable dogma. *Yangban* values and conduct began to be examined. The doctrines of Chu-Hsi's Neo-Confucianism began to be explored critically, as scholars studied the system of thought propounded by another Chinese philosopher, Wang Yang-ming. Some scholars, for example Yun Hyu, Pak Se-dang and Chŏng Yagyong, turned to the past in an attempt to rediscover the original essence of Confucian thought. Pak Se-dang went further, even offering fresh interpretations of Taoist thought through his study of *Lao-Tzu* and *Chuang-tzu*.

There were also responses to economic growth, social change and the introduction of Western ideas. These new developments

Tongguk-yŏ Chido, a Korean map, early 18th century.

led scholars to break away from the abstractions and rigidity of Neo-Confucian doctrine and search for practical solutions and responses to the new social and technological situation. The result was an incredible surge of interest in all forms of practical scholarship (*Sirhak*). Large numbers of texts were produced in areas as diverse as agriculture, politics, economics, history, culture and technology.

During the latter half of the 18th century, in Chŏngjo's reign, interest in Catholicism increased enormously. The common people were much attracted to Catholicism's tenet that all people are equal, while scholars saw the religion as a useful counterbalance to the grasping and predatory nature of the Chosŏn state and the rigidity of Neo-Confucian orthodoxy. By the 18th century there were tens of thousands of believers. In the history of the Catholic church, there is no other instance of churches being formed before the actual arrival of priests. Chŏngjo himself considered the pursuit of equality by the common people as equally important as his own secret plan for abolishing slavery, and did not regard Catholicism as a dangerous influence. His religious toleration led to his downfall, however, as those bureaucrats in power saw Catholicism as a pernicious doctrine, contrary to Neo-Confucianism and subversive of the state.

The 19th century to 1864

Political instability and corruption

When Chŏngjo died in 1800, he was succeeded by his son, a mere ten-year old boy. As a result, power passed to the boy's father-in-law, Kim Cho-sun of the Andong Kim clan. For most of the rest of the century control was entirely in the hands of this clan, their hold being broken for a time only to be replaced by that of another royal in-law family, the P'ungyang Cho clan.

As the in-law families rose to power, so the policy of impartiality in appointing government officials was lost. Bribery became rife as all levels of officials, especially those in local administration, sought to secure posts for themselves. This in turn led to widespread corruption as officials strove both to recover the losses they sustained in offering bribes and to line their own pockets further.

In local administration, county magistrates and *hyangni* alike use the three sources of government revenue, land tax, military cloth tax and grain loans to extract money from the hapless peasants. With respect to the land tax the common people found themselves taxed on abandoned fields, subjected to excessive surcharges and handling fees, and forced to make payments over and above the fixed amounts decided by central government. Officials abused the military cloth tax system by making illegal exactions such as levying the cloth tax on the deceased, and profited from the grain loan system by charging extremely high interest on loans.

The result of such corruption was grinding poverty on the part of the peasants. Many lost their land and were forced to sell their services as tenant farmers or, worse, agricultural wage labourers. Some fled to become mine workers. During times of famine, poor farmers would abandon their land for the hills and try to eke out a living practising slash and burn agriculture. Even there, they could not escape the tax demands of local officials. Still others gave up altogether and embarked upon a life of wandering.

Corruption in the local administration threatened not only the livelihood of the peasants but also the fiscal soundness of central government, as more and more tax revenue found its way into the hands of local officials. In an attempt to combat the decay the central government despatched secret inspectors to locate and report corruption in the countryside. The effect of this measure was limited, however. It served as a restraining factor but could not eliminate the problem.

Breakdown of the Chosŏn class system

The social structure of Chosŏn, on the surface rigidly specified and maintained by hereditary factors, was, at bottom, underpinned by vast differentials in the distribution of wealth. In the 17th and 18th centuries, the distribution of wealth began to change and cross class boundaries. Such change brought with it a gradual breakdown of the traditional status system. In the 19th century, this trend continued.

The numbers of fallen *yangban* steadily increased. The *chungin* improved their position, amassing wealth through private trading activities and thus increasing their influence in society. The provincial gentry started to grow in strength and produce more and more successful candidates in the higher civil service examinations. Numbers of peasants rose to become rich farmers. As social boundaries became blurred, it was increasingly more difficult to maintain a distinction between freemen and slaves. Slavery had been slowly decreasing in the 17th and 18th centuries and in 1801, all public slavery was abolished (although private slaves continued to be owned).

As a caveat to the above, it must not be assumed that the increase in social mobility heralded the disappearance of all class distinctions. The difference from previous times is one of degree, not of kind. The upper classes strove hard to maintain their position, and even now Korean society is markedly elitist and stratified.

Kim Tae-gŏn, (1822-1846) the first catholic priest in Korea.

Ch'ŏnjushilŭi, an exposition of the catholic faith.

Movements for change

The peasants' struggle for survival

In response to the difficulties they faced in the form of famine and heavy taxes, many peasants migrated to the *Chien-tao*, (*Kando*: Korean) region of Manchuria or the Russian maritime Province. Others remained to demonstrate their unrest, at first in covert, later in more open ways. Slogans began to appear more and more in public places, denouncing local government corruption. Later, a number of peasants turned to brigandage. Soon, they became better organised as smaller bands joined together, and within a short period of time, there were open rebellions, usually led by discontented *yangban*. In 1811, the Hong Kyŏng-nae Rebellion broke out, to be followed in 1862 by an uprising in Chinju. In addition to these large scale uprisings, there was a host of minor ones, all over the country. These early uprisings were local in character and their force was soon spent.

Another way in which the peasants sought to survive their mistreatment was through religion. In the countryside, a new religion started to gain popularity. *Tonghak* (Eastern

Chŏe Che-u, the founder of Tonghak

Learning) was taken from many different sources: Confucianism, Buddhism, Taoism, Catholicism and shamanism. It held great appeal for the peasants, calling for equality for all and reforms of government and society. Its popularity proved so great that the government perceived it as a serious threat. Accordingly, its founder, Ch'oe Che-u was arrested in 1863 on charges of misleading the people and sowing discord in society, and he was executed the following year. His death sent many of his followers into hiding and there was a temporary lull in the strength of the movement. Thirty years later, however, *Tonghak* would revive in the name of political freedom and open rebellion would break out.

The further spread of Catholicism

The fortunes of Catholicism in the public eye rose and fell as power came to be held by different groups. In 1801, it was persecuted because of the threat it posed to Chosŏn's social and political order. Once the Andong Kim took control of the government, it enjoyed a period of toleration. When the P'ung-yang Cho clan came to power, it was again persecuted, from 1839 to 1846, and tolerated again upon the return of the Andong Kim in 1849.

Catholicism spread rapidly as its creed of equality meshed perfectly with the breakdown of the status system and appealed to various sectors of society. Commoners quickly became believers, because the Catholic creed of equality, that everyone is a child of God, appealed to them. Women became followers for the same reason. It gave them hope that they could be free from the yoke of subordination to men. The middle classes could also find justification in the religion for their new place in society.

KOREA AND THE INTERNATIONAL STAGE: 1864-1910.

Kanghwado Island. Korean resistance to contact with the West.

Korea the international stage

Isolationism Pressure by Western Power

Complications in the order of succession led to a twelve-year-old, Kojong, ascending to the throne in 1864. His father, Hŭngsŏn Taewon-gun, assumed control. The Taewon-gun tried to strengthen the country, both politically and economically. His policy was to exert total control over the country from the throne. He therefore set about to destroy the influence of the powerful noble families, especially the Andong Kim. Once again, a policy of appointment of officials from different colours was instigated.

In addition to this, the policy was broadened to include people from lesser backgrounds. Thus control was removed from the select few; appointments were to be made on merit; it may be argued that the Taewon-gun was the first absolute monarch since the death of Sejo, whose aims were similar in many ways.

In the eighteen-thirties and-forties, British and French vessels had appeared off the coast of Korea seeking to establish trade. Under the Taewon-gun, Korea's isolationist policy was even more strongly enforced

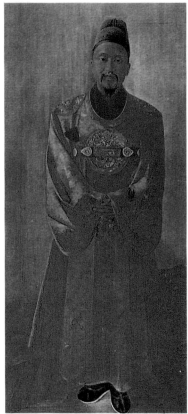

A life-size Portrait of Emperor Kojong, painted in 1899 by Hubert Voss.

and the foreign ships being regarded as yet another threat to the already troubled kingdom. The Taewon-gun thought that Korea was simply not strong enough to deal with the foreign menace, especially in the light of what had happened in China as a result of contact with the Western trading nations.

To protect the country further against Western influences, the Taewon-gun ordered the suppression of Catholicism. This led to French military reprisals in 1866 in the first of a series of "Foreign Disturbances". Later, in 1871, an American expedition was repulsed. None of these expeditions was well-planned, nor had any long-term aim. The only result was that the Taewon-gun strengthened his isolationist policy, including his anti-Japanese stance. Japan was, at the time, the only major power which had any clear desire to force Korea to open its doors for trade.

Korea's isolationist policy was finally abandoned when the Taewon-gun was forced to relinquish control in 1873. One reason was that there had already been a powerful pro-Western group in the government for many years. In particular, representatives from the *Sirhak* school of thought argued that Korea would have to have trade and contact with other nations in order to become rich and technologically advanced. The major cause of the Taewon-gun's retirement was that he himself had created a new politically powerful family: the Yŏhŭng Min. The wife of the young king was from this family and she took the opportunity to force the retirement of the Taewon-gun in the light of much criticism of him by members of her family and Confucian officials. One particular complaint was about his anti-Confucian policies in the countryside. The rural-based literati resented any attacks on their academies, which were their power bases.

The Japanese were able to take advantage of the lull in isolationism by stage-managing a minor international incident and thereby negotiating for themselves a favourable treaty, known as the ''1876 Treaty of Friendship'' or ''Treaty of Kanghwa''. This treaty is important for a number of reasons. It provided the Japanese with the access to the ports of Korea needed for their aggressive economic and political policies towards the Kingdom; secondly, by acknowledging Korea as an independent nation the Japanese were able to deny any rights of protection to the Chinese; and thirdly, by granting itself the right to explore Korean territorial waters, Japan was able to counter Russian expansionism southwards. In short, the Treaty of Kanghwa brought Korea out of its shell and onto the international, imperial scene.

Shrine dedicated to Queen Min.

With greater contact available, a pro-Japanese group began to emerge in the government. King Kojong was able to exploit new ideas for reform based on ideas from missions which had been sent, not only to Japan but also to Ching China. Reforms were made in the military and administrative structures of Korea. As a reaction against foreign ideas and influences, another group made its feelings felt. This was a more traditional

group of members of the literati who now, ironically, looked to the Taewon-gun as a true leader of Confucian Korea. The Taewon-gun finally came back to power as the result of an anti-Japanese military rebellion in 1882, and dismantled many of the more progressive attempts at modernization.

The Taewon-gun's revival of isolationist Korea was short-lived, however. The Japanese reacted to events by showing a willingness to use military force if necessary; Ching China responded by sending a large army into Korea to exercise its right to control matters Korean, and abducted the Taewon-gun. As he was regarded as the leader of the mutiny, the Taewon-gun's disappearance from the political scene meant that the government could re-enter into negotiations with the Japanese. Japan and China were thus competing for influence in the Korean government. As a result of Chinese influence, Korea signed treaties with several Western nations, this being a way of lessening Japanese influence over the peninsula.

With the Taewon-gun in China, the political scene was dominated by the pro-Ching family of Min, the royal in-laws. There was, however, considerable influence exerted by a newly-formed "Progressive Party", whose pro-Japanese stance was not altogether supported by that country. In a *coup d'état* organised by the progressives in 1884, the main demand made was for the return of the Taewon-gun from China. This was perceived as the only way of breaking the power of the Min family and its pro-Chinese policy. The coup was finally put down by Chinese forces.

The Taewon-gun was finally returned to Korea, not due to internal pressures, but as an attempt to counter an increasing Russian imperial presence in the peninsula. The Russian Minister, Karl Waeber, had managed to create an anti-Ching lobby in the government, and even the King and Queen were leaning more towards a pro-Russian standpoint. It was not only China that feared Russian designs, however. The threat of Russian influence in Korea prompted the British to occupy Kŏmun-do, an island situated in a strategic position off the southern coast. But they were forced to withdraw after both Russian and Chinese reaction to the event. It had thus become clear that not even the Taewon-gun was in position to restore Korean isolationism; the great powers were clearly not going to leave the country to its own devices.

The Russian Legation (late 19th century).

The Tonghak Movement

*T*onghak (Eastern Learning) had been quietly taking shape in the countryside during the thirty years since the execution of its founder, Ch'oe Che-u. In 1892 there were gatherings, which were violently dispersed, calling for the reinstatement of Ch'oe and an end to foreign interference in Korea. The peasantry's hatred of *yangban* misrule was compounded by the suffering caused by the trading habits of foreign, especially Japanese merchants. By this time, Japan was the source of half of Korea's imports, while approximately ninety percent of its exports went to Japan. The Korean peasants were in no position to cope with the sharp practices of the Japanese traders.

In 1894, open rebellion broke out. A badly-equipped army emerged from the countryside, made up of all sorts of different rural people. The disgruntled peasantry were led by fallen *yangban*, the middle classes also joined this improvised army. At its peak, its numbers rose to more than ten thousand. After early successes against government forces, the *Tonghak* movement forced the government to negotiate a truce. Their demands were an end to the misrule of the country and an end to the exploitation by foreign powers. At this point the *Tonghak* were in an extremely strong position, and were establishing their control over more and more of the country.

Although the structure of *Tonghak* was religious, its practice was political and its aims clear. As congregations were established in village after village, stronger and stronger attempts were made to wipe out exploitation by local administrators. It was a fight for the rights of the people. It was also nationalistic in the sense that those who collaborated with the Japanese were to be punished.

The *Tonghak* uprising was so appealing, especially to the peasantry, that the government was forced to ask the Chinese for assistance in putting down the revolt. In response to this the Japanese sent a large contingent of troops to the country. A treaty was signed which granted rule to the *Tonghak* over part of the south of the country. However, in July 1894, the Sino-Japanese war broke out. The *Tonghak* army rose again, this time against the foreign forces. Resistance con-

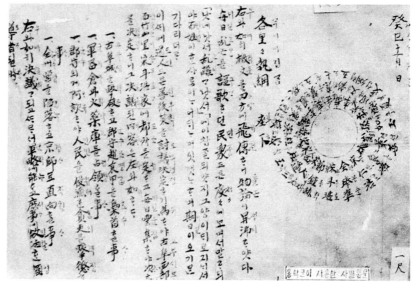

A document used by Tonghak forces.

tinued for five months before the war was finally defeated by a combined force of government and Japanese troops.

Japan's position of influence was becoming stronger, both with the defeat of the *Tonghak* forces and the Japanese victory in the war against China. Although Japan was prevented from taking full advantage of its victory by Western powers, it was in a sufficiently strong position in Korea to demand social and administrative reforms throughout the kingdom. In particular, many class distinctions were abolished and local governments reorganized. The reforms of 1894 certainly

modernized the structure of Korean society, but they also made it even easier for the Japanese to invade the economy. In addition, there was to be no strengthening of the Korean military. The Taewon-gun and his Confucian faction opposed the reforms bitterly. Ultimately he was forced to retire altogether from the political stage by the newly-appointed Japanese representative, Inoue. Japan's influence over Korean politics was further extended when Inoue's successor organized the assassination of Queen Min, whose pro-Russian leanings were posing a threat to Japanese interests.

JAPANESE COLONIZATION:1910-1945

Chinese influence in Korea had been lost after the Sino-Japanese war of 1894-5. As a result of the Boxer rebellion in 1900, China's position was further weakened; in particular, the Russians had occupied part of Manchuria, thus also posing a threat to Japanese interests. By playing on Western imperial fears, the Japanese managed to negotiate agreements with first Britain, then the United States with regard to foreign policy in the Far East. The most important consequence of these agreements was in the recognition of Japan's interests in Korea. Her victories in the Russo-Japanese war of 1904-5 meant that, finally, Japan was free to do as she pleased with the Korean peninsula.

Although forced to abandon plans to control uncultivated state land, the Japanese had managed to penetrate most of the important government departments. To help their fight against the Russians, the Japanese started work on building railway and other communication systems. The following year a new treaty was signed, despite bitter opposition, which effectively put the entire administration in the hands of the Japanese. This treaty is referred to as the "Protectorate Treaty" or, more commonly, "The Treaty of 1905". It was sealed by force, without the consent of the King or his ministers, and effectively marks the end of Korean control over their own internal affairs.

Despite Korean attempts to gather international support, the Japanese were able to take over complete control over the peninsula, step by step. In 1907, Kojong was forced to abdicate the throne to his son, Sunjong. Violent protests were put down by force and Japanese control was tightened. The Korean army was reduced to a token force and finally disbanded when the remaining troops turned on the Japanese. In 1910, a new governor was appointed who was responsible for the final annexation. Publication of newspapers was suspended and patriotic organizations were closed down. Leading dissident figures were arrested and all police functions were taken over by an enlarged Japanese police force. The Prime Minister, Yi Wan Yong, assured himself a place in history by putting his name to the annexation agreement. The last king was finally forced to abdicate and Korea became a colony of Japan.

Colonial Rule

Despite opposition, both ideological and military, the Japanese remained in complete control of the Korean Peninsula until the end of the Second World War. Japanese rule was based entirely on self-interest, both in Korea and its other colony, Taiwan. Thus, although progress was made in some fields, most notably transport, developments were designed to aid the Japanese in their period of expansionism. Economically, Koreans became worse off after 1910, despite massive investment by Japanese companies and quasi-governmental bodies. Rice cultivation was increased, but the large land-owners were the only ones who benefited. After annexation, something like 50 percent of Korea's rice harvest went to Japan. Similarly, the production of industrial goods and other products increased, but the profits went to the investors; the Japanese companies who had taken over the economy.

It is not too much of an exaggeration to say that Korea was used as a work-house for Japanese interests. Roads and railways were built to aid the military in any movements

"Righteous armies": public resistence to Japanese rule towards the end of the Chosŏn Dynasty.

against China; laborers were locally recruited and many hundreds of thousands more were forcibly deported to Japan. In both manufacturing industries and agriculture, the life of the workers was difficult in the extreme. On the land, many were reduced to the level of tenant farmers, working for absentee Japanese landlords and living at a subsistence level only. In the factories, hours were long and pay minimal.

Resistance to Occupation

During the final years of the 19th century, opposition to foreign influence grew, not only in the government. The Independence Club was formed in 1896, consisting of various governmental and public figures, including Sŏ Chae-p'il (Philip Jaisohn) who was responsible for the publication of *The Independent* that same year. *The Independent* was a bilingual newspaper, published in *hangŭl* and English, and served as a public mouthpiece for the views of the Independence Club. This group's political views were derived, in part, from *Sirhak* and were nationalistic in spirit but modern in nature. As a result of the reforms called for in the pages of *The Independent,* Russian influence in Seoul was reduced. Unfortunately, the thoughts of the Independence Club were a little too appealing to the public; it became too much of a threat to the administration. Public meetings were violently broken up and the club was finally dissolved.

Following on from the ideas of the Independence Club, many other political associations were formed prior to annexation. During this period, most of the demands were for the reduction of Japanese influence in Korea. One such organization was called the Korea Preservation Society, or Poanhoe, formed in 1904. It started out by calling for a stop to Japanese takeover of state land. In this, it was successful, but it too was disbanded as it became too broadly anti-Japanese. Another group, again arguing for Korean independence and internal reform, was called the

Society for the Study of Constitutional Government or Hŏnjŏng Yŏn-guhoe. This, and other societies, demanded internal strength and the right societies were dissolved and many of their leaders were arrested as the Japanese police state began to make itself more and more strongly felt.

Not all resistance to the Japanese was peaceful, though. When the Korean Army was disbanded in 1907, many former soldiers turned to guerrilla warfare, attacking Japanese garrisons and destroying lines of communication. These "Righte-

ous Armies" were a younger brother of the Tonghak Army; Confucian literati and peasantry offered armed but sporadic resistance to the occupying forces. When the Korean Army was disbanded the guerilla ranks nearly doubled. With trained military men amongst them, their effectiveness soared, reaching a peak of activity in 1908. Thousands of them died in their struggle against the Japanese, and resistance continued, even after annexation, from émigré Korean areas in Manchuria and the Russian Maritime Territory.

Tongnipmun, Gate of Independence, in Seoul.

The March First Movement

King Kojong, who was forced off the throne in 1907, died in 1919. As preparations for his funeral were being made, nationalist leaders saw the perfect opportunity for organized, largescale demonstrations against the Japanese. Originally the plan was to hold the demonstrations on March 3, the day of the funeral, but fearing word of their plan would be leaked, the leaders moved the date on which they planned to sign a Declaration of Independence ahead two days and the anniversary of the movement is celebrated on March 1.

Thirty-three men signed the document and through their religious organizations, primarily Christian and Ch'ŏndo-gyo, copies of the Declaration were read throughout the Peninsula and students as well as thousands of other people flowed into the streets shouting, "Long live Korean independence!" The Japanese were surprised by the sudden outcry and the depth of support. The Japanese react-

ed by killing over 7,000, injuring over 15,000, and arresting over 40,000. The Japanese admitted this level of violence in their own reports. They also destroyed 415 homes, two schools, and 47 churches. In at least one case, one church was burned with its congregation trapped inside.

In spite of the scale of the demonstrations, they were not successful in driving out the Japanese. Although the demonstrations were reported overseas, and although many Koreans hoped Woodrow Wilson's doctrine of selfdetermination of nations would apply to them, in the end the Japanese, allied with the other victors of World War I, were too powerful to be forced out.

The proclamation of Korean Independence in 1919 and the Statue of the Independence Movement.

Provisional Government in China

The March First Declaration was read in major cities around the world where Koreans were living in exile. After the initial failure of the March First Movement, Korean exiles in Shanghai created the Provisional Government of the Republic of Korea in April 1919. One of its leading figures was Syngman Rhee who later moved to Hawaii and then returned to Korea after World War II to become the first president. The Provisional Government had representatives from all 13 of the Korean provinces. Although their power weakened as Japan prepared for World War II, they continued to perform governmental functions including recruitment of troops to fight with the allies against Japan.

Japanese Colonial Policy

After the March First Movement and the failure of the Japanese to anticipate such an event, the Japanese changed their approach from a heavy-handed, military-dominated policy to one of so-called enlightenment. They allowed Korean publications of newspapers and literary works in *hangŭl*. Japanese controls remained in place, however, and the newspapers were heavily censored. The somewhat open policy was gradually abandoned as the Japanese war machine moved into Manchuria in 1931 and on into China after 1937.

As the war spread, Japan began to demand more and more from Korea. For example, a larger portion of the essential rice crop was exported to Japan even though many Koreans did not have enough rice to eat. Conditions for farmers and other workers became so bad that many fled Korea, fleeing to Manchuria or Japan or other countries to find a way to make a living. The Japanese employed many low-skilled laborers in conditions that closely resembled slavery.

The urban-industrial sector did not fare any better than did the agricultural sector. As economic conditions worsened, the controls of the Japanese tightened. The Japanese police grew in power, numbers and diversity. Thought police began to insure that all the emperors's subjects were loyal in word and deed. Koreans were forced to learn Japanese in school, and were eventually forbidden to use Korean. One of the most striking tragedies was the loss of their own surnames. Koreans had to give up their names and take on Japanese-style names.

The key members of the Korean Provisional Government in exile in Shanghai.

DIVISION AND THE ESTABLISHMENT OF THE REPUBLIC OF KOREA: 1945-PRESENT.

A special ceremony inaugurating the Republic of Korea Government on August 15, 1948

Ideological Divisions

During the 20s various opposition groups formed clandestinely to fight against the Japanese. Some of these groups were Communist; others were nationalistic. In 1927 a coalition of the two approaches was attempted. A new organization called the Sin-ganhoe (The New Stem Association), was formed. They demanded that the Japanese government cease to exclude Korean children from schools, withdraw exploitative agencies, and improve educational policies. Factions within the organization and Japanese pressure from without eventually forced its dissolution.

Just before the end of World War II, the Provisional Government attempted to bring leftists into their organization and form a kind of coalition government, but this attempt, too, was to be short-lived. On December 1, 1943, the Allies met in Cairo and issued a declaration, part of which called for an independent Korea.

The end of the war in August 1945, found the Russians, having already participated in the defeat of the Germans, moving quickly toward Japan. The United States on the other hand was completely occupied with affairs in Japan. The war had ended sooner than anyone anticipated because of the atomic bomb and thus the United States did not have an occupational army strategy developed. In haste, and in an effort to stop the advance of the Russians, a line at the 38th parallel was determined to be the point beyond which Russians would not advance. The United States slowly moved to take up its responsibilities of resettling Koreans returning from abroad and otherwise trying to develop a government for the Korean Peninsula. In December of that year, ministers of the United States, the Soviet Union, and

Great Britain met in Moscow and decided to put Korea under a trusteeship in their care in preparation for unification. Initially, all parties in Korea opposed the action, but under orders from Moscow, the Communists changed their position to one of support for the trusteeship.

The United States and the Soviet Union met in January 1946 to implement the Moscow Agreement whereupon the Russians proposed that all parties who disagreed with the trusteeship be excluded, which would of course leave the government in the hands of the pro-Moscow group. The United States submitted that all parties in Korea, whether they agreed with the trusteeship or not, should be considered. The meetings broke off in an impasse. Confusion reigned internally with several leaders in the South and North vying for power. The two superpowers did not meet again for another year, May 1947, at which point their positions remained the same. The United States proposed a U.N. supervised election in the North and the South, and although the U.N. accepted the proposal, U.N. observers were not allowed in the North. The South went ahead with an election process,

electing an assembly with seats filled for southern provinces and unfilled for northern provinces, and the elected assembly elected a president, Syngman Rhee, who led the new govenrment into a constitutional assembly and finally to the promulgation of the Republic of Korea on August 15, 1948. The North followed by declaring their Communist government shortly thereafter.

The Korean War

The Republic of Korea had a larger population because traditionally more people lived in the south, but also hordes of refugees fled to the South from the Communist government in the North. But the northern government had more arms and was capable of uniting the Peninsula by force. As an example, the South had not a single tank, yet the Russians had supplied the North with 242 tanks.

On Sunday morning, June 25, 1950, the northern army struck deeply across the 38th parallel and moved into Seoul and on south-ward. They pushed the southern army and a few American advisors in front of them, capturing many including an American general. Finally, on the outskirts of Pusan, just before the northern army pushed the remaining defenders into the ocean, the United Nations sponsored a special command unifying 16 allies under the command of General Douglas MacArthur. MacArthur's decisive West Coast landing in the tidal flats at Inch'ŏn cut the northern army's advance in two. In September, the U.N. troops retook Seoul and started marching north. They took P'yŏngyang and marched on to the Chinese border.

The newly communized Chinese government sent large numbers of troops to rescue their northern ally and the U.N. forces beat a hasty, but costly retreat. The Communists retook Seoul on january 4, 1951, but the capital changed hands for the fourth and final time on March 12, when the U.N. Forces again retook the city. The two sides fought on for high ground here and there along the 38th parallel until an armistice was signed on July 27, 1953. A demilitarized zone was declared and both sides continue to meet from time to time at the border village called P'anmunjŏm.

Democratic Revolution

Syngman Rhee remained President throughout the war and for several years thereafter, but corruption and economic stagnation bred discontent. Finally, with the blatant ballot box stuffing and other fraudulent election practices in the spring of 1960, demonstrations, initially led by students but soon joined by citizens from all walks of life, led to the resignation of the old patriot. He left Korea and died in exile where he had spent most of his life.

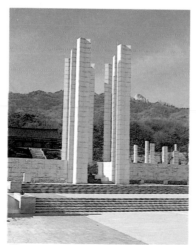

The pagoda commemorating the 1960 movement for democracy.

The Second, Third and Fourth Republics

For about a year after Syngman Rhee's departure the democratic process left Korea with a new President, Yun Po-sun, and Prime Minister, Chang Myon, under the Second Republic, but social chaos grew. On May 16, 1961, a two-star general, Park Chung-Hee, led a military coup and took over the control of the government, initially leading a group of military officers in a military junta. The military officers soon took off their uniforms and proceeded to lead Korea into what is called its Third, and later its Fourth, Republic. In spite of its difficult beginning, the new government set its sights on economic development and subsequently led the country through some of the most remarkable economic growth ever seen on this planet. Whereas most countries never see their GNP grow by 10 percent in a single year, Korea in the 70s averaged nearly 10 percent each year.

The Fifth and Sixth Republics

With the assassination of President Park Chung Hee on October 26, 1979, the then-Prime Minister, Choi Kyu-hah, succeeded the presidency to take over the caretaker government. He was replaced by two-star general Chun Doo Hwan as the Fifth Republic came into being. The Fifth Republic carried out a series of social reforms and in the economic sector, registered the first-ever surplus in the balance of payments in the history of the Republic. Chun Doo Hwan was succeeded by Roh Tae Woo who won the direct presidential election following the revision of the Constitution. With the Sixth Republic thus launched, there was a steady transition from authoritarianism to democracy. This was followed by the merger of three major political parties to form a solid majority in the National Assembly with a view to continuing the drive towards democracy. Noteworthy was the success of 'Northern Diplomacy,' highlighted by the opening of diplomatic relations with the Soviet Union and the People's Republic of China. Korea's acceptance in world politics as a significant international state was shown by the fact that the 24th Olympiad was held in Seoul in 1988—the most successful of any games held to that time in terms of the number and scale of participating countries. Korea took fourth place in the gold medal count, after the Soviet Union, East Germany and the United States.

New Era of Civilian Rule

In a completely free and fair election in 1992, Kim Young Sam became the first civilian chief executive in 32 years. Upon assuming office on February 25, 1993, President Kim carried out bold reform policies to build a New Korea. Initial reform measures involved the reorganization of the military and the intelligence agencies to end their meddling in politics. The four major goals of the new administration are a clean government, a sound economy, a healthy society and peaceful unification. For a clean government, high-ranking public officials are required to register and make public their personal assets to discourage illegal accumulation of wealth under the Public Officials' Ethics Law. To promote clean politics and participatory democracy, a package of three political reform bills was unanimously passed by the National Assembly in 1994—the Law for Electing Public Officials and Preventing Electoral Irregularities, the Political Fund Law and the Local Autonomy Law. A sound economy means a New Economy free of unwarranted controls and protection—an economy which guarantees self-regulation and fair competition and encourages the private initiative and creativity necessary for economic revitalization. Under the New Economy, a real-name system for all financial transactions was implemented in August 1993 to assist in the realization of economic justice and clean government. For peaceful unification, President Kim stressed in his inaugural address that what is needed is not emotionalism but a reasoned national consensus on achieving this crucial goal. Basic principles for unification are: 1) independence based on the wishes and inherent capability of the Korean people, 2) peace without the use of force or the overthrow of the other side, and 3) democracy based on freedom and the sovereign rights of all Koreans. Under these principles, the unification formula for the Korean National Community envisages the following three phases:

1) Reconciliation and Cooperation: The present hostility and confrontation will be replaced with reconciliation and cooperation.

2) Korean Commonwealth: Once peaceful coexistence and co-prosperity is secured, the two parts of Korea shall be joined in a single socio-economic community.

3) Single Nation-State: This phase will be completed with full integration of the South and the North.

In the light of global trends toward universal freedom, welfare and openness, the Kim administration is striving to promote the well-being of the entire Korean people with the sincere hope that North Korea will pursue reform and openness under conditions of stability for peaceful unification.

President Kim Young Sam taking the oath of office on February 25, 1993.

The Prime Ministers of South and North Korea exchanging an intra-Korean agreement on September 19, 1992.

SUGGESTED FURTHER READING

General

Han Wook-keun. *The History of Korea.* Translated by Kyong-shik Lee, edited by Grafton K. Mintz. Honolulu: University Press of Hawaii, 1971.

Hatada, Takashi. *A History of Korea.* Translated and edited by Warren W. Smith, Jr. and Benjamin H. Hazard. Santa Barbara: ABC Clio, 1969.

Henthorn, William E. *A History of Korea.* New York: Free Press, 1971.

Hulbert, Homer B. *The History of Korea.* 2 vols. Edited by Clarence N. Weems. New York: Hilary House, 1962.

Joe, Wanne J. *Traditional Korea: A Cultural History.* Seoul: Chungang Univerity Press, 1972.

Lee Ki-baik. *A New History of Korea.* Seoul: Ilchokak, 1984.

Nahm, Andrew C. *A Panorama of 5000 Years: Korean History.* Seoul: Hollym International Corp., 1986.

Rutt, Richard. *James Scarth Gale's History of the Korean People.* Seoul: Royal Asiatic Society, 1975.

Sohn Pow-key, Kim Chol-choon and Hong Yi-sup. *The History of Korea.* Seoul: Korean National Commission for UNESCO, 1970.

Ancient

Covell, Jon Carter and Alan Covell. *Korean Impact on Japanese Culture: Japan's Hidden History.* Seoul: Hollym International Corp., 1985.

Gardiner, K.H.J. *The Early History of Korea: The Historical Development of the Peninsula Up to the Introduction of Buddhism in the Fourth Century A.D.* Honolulu: University of Hawaii Press, 1969.

International Cultural Foundation. *Upper-Class Culture in Yi-Dynasty Korea.* Seoul: Si-sayong-o-sa, Inc. 1982.

Iryŏn. *Samguk Yusa: Legends and History of the Three Kingdoms of Ancient Korea.* Translated by Tae-Hung Ha and Grafton K. Mintz. Seoul: Yonsei University Press, 1972.

Kang, Hugh H.W., ed. *The Traditional Culture and Society of Korea: Thought and Institutions.* Honolulu: Center for Korean Studies, Univ. of Hawaii, 1975.

Kim Jeong-hak. *The Prehistory of Korea.* Translated by Richard J. Pearson and Kazue Pearson, Honolulu: University Press of Hawaii, 1979.

King Sejong the Great. Seoul: King Sejong Memorial Society. 1981.

Ledyard, Gari. *The Dutch Come to Korea.* Seoul: Royal Asiatic Society, 1971.

Meskill, John. *Ch'oe Pu's Diary: A Record of Drifting Across the Sea.* Tucson: University of Arizona Press, 1965.

Park Yune-hee. *Admiral Yi Sun-shin and His Turtleboat Armada.* Revised edition. Seoul: Hanjin Publishing Co., 1978.

Wagner, Edward W. *The Literati Purges: Political Conflict in Early Yi Korea.* Cambridge, Mass.: East Asian Research Center, Harvard University, 1974.

Modern (to 1945)

Choe Ching Young. *The Rule of the Taewŏn'gun, 1864-1873: Restoration in Yi Korea.* Cambridge, Mass.: East Asian Research Center, Harvard University, 1972.

Cook, Harold F. *Korea's 1884 Incident: Its Background and Kim Ok-Kyun's Elusive Dream.* Seoul: Taewon Publishing Co., 1972.

Dallet, Charles. *Historie de l'Église de Corée.* Paris: V. Palme, 1874. 2 vols. Reprint, Seoul: Royal Asistic Society, 1975.

Dennett, Tyler. *Americans in Eastern Asia: A Critical Study of the policy of the United States with Reference to China, Japan and Korea in the Nineteenth Century.* New york: Macmillan, 1922. Reprint. New York: Barnes and Noble, 1963.

Deuchler, Martina. *Confucian Gentlemen and Barbarian Envoys: The Opening of Korea, 1875-1885.* Seattle: University of Washington press, 1977.

Grajdanzev, Andrew J. *Modern Korea.* New York: Institute of Pacific Relations, 1944. Reprint. Seoul: Royal Asiatic Society,1975.

Hulbert, Homer B. *The Passing of Korea.* New York: Doubleday Page, 1906, Reprint. Seoul: Yonsei University Press, 1969.

Kim, C.I. Eugene and Han-Kyo Kim. *Korea and the Politics of Imperialism, 1876-1910.* Berkeley and Los Angeles: University of California Press, 1967.

Kim Key-Hiuk. *The Last Phase of the East Asian World Order: Korea, Japan, and the Chinese Empire, 1860-1882.* Berkeley: University of California Press, 1980.

Lee Chong-sik. *The Politics of Korean Nationalism,* Berkeley: University of California Press, 1965.

McKenzie, Frederick A. *Korea's Fight for Freedom.* New York: Revell, 1920. Reprint. Seoul: Yonsei University Press, 1969.

____. *The Tragedy of Korea.* London: Hodder and Strongton, 1908. Reprint. Seoul: Yonsei University Press, 1969.

Nahm, Andrew C., ed. *American-Korean Relations 1866-1976. The United States and Korea.* Kalamazoo: Western Michigan University, 1979.

____. ed. *Korean under Japanese Colonial Ruel: Studies of the Policy and Techniques of Japanese Colonialism.* Kalamazoo: Center for Korean Studies, Western Michigan University, 1973.

Palais, James B. *Politics and Policy in Traditional Korea.* Cambridge, Mass.: Harvard University, 1975.

Suh Dae-sook and Chae-jin Lee, ed. *Political Leadership in Korea.* Seattle: University of Washington Press, 1975.

Weems, Benjamin B. *Reform, Rebellion and the Heavenly Way.* Tucson: University of Arizona Press, 1964.

CULTURE

PHILOSOPHY AND RELIGION

Over the centuries, Korea has been subject to a number of diverse religious and philosophical influences. Shamanism, the indigenous religion, first appeared in the peninsula in Neolithic times. Buddhism and Confucianism were introduced from foreign sources in the fourth century AD (as was Taoism, a minor influence). In the eighteenth century Catholicism came from the West, to be followed by Protestantism in the late nineteenth century.

As each of these influences was introduced it took on a character peculiar to Korea. Buddhism absorbed many Shamanistic rituals and developed a new sect in which both the textual and sudden enlightenment schools were reconciled. Confucianism also absorbed Shamanism to some degree, and was elevated to the status of an absolute, unquestionable orthodoxy for social and private conduct. Catholicism and Protestantism are pursued with a fervour which would surprise all but the most charismatic of Christians in Western congregations.

Though many Koreans adhere exclusively to one belief system, some see no contradiction in subscribing to all. In general, the everyday lives of Koreans are influenced by all of the country's belief systems, as their piecemeal acceptance has come to permeate the whole of society. However, we may safely say that the doctrines of Neo-Confucianism play the major role in determining social structure and individual action.

A model of Sŏnangdang, a pile of stones at the entrance of a village to pray for good luck—a shamanist shrine.

When disaster befalls a Korean household all good housewives know where to go. They consult a Shaman to seek a cure for lingering illness, when a husband takes a mistress and to resolve family quarrels. They go to learn about a prospective son or daughter-in-law and when examinations are imminent. They go whether they are Buddhist, Confucian or Christian. They go because Shamanism is the thread which runs through the cloth of Korean society, colouring its other religions, its art, its music and dance.

Shamanism is the folk worship of a pantheon of household, village, animate and inanimate forces in nature through a female medium or Shaman. Shaman *kut* or exorcisms are still very much alive in Korea today. although visitors to Korea would indeed be fortunate to witness a *kut* first hand, evidence of Shamanism is all around. Throughout the countryside one can see Shaman "spirit posts" and bright cloth tied to trees, all placed to repel evil spirits or placate the gods of nature. Shaman symbols, including the most popular, the crane, are used to decorate all manner of household articles from cups to quilts; and the dragon, tiger, phoenix, or and turtle are commonly seen on roof-tiles and doorways to keep evil spirits from entering.

Modern Koreans have ambivalent feelings about Shamanism. On the one hand they are embarrassed by the superstitious nature of Shamanism which they feel is out of place in such a rapidly-developing nation. On the other they recognize that Shamanism is a uniquely Korean form of religious and artistic expression. Indeed, universities and folklore associations increasingly sponsor public performances of *kut* or Shaman dancing as an educational and entertaining display of Korea's cultural heritage.

Shamanism is believed to have entered the peninsula with the Altaic settlers from the north deep in Korea's prehistoric past. Whatever its origins, Shaman rituals have been shaped by centuries of Korean history. Korean Shamanism benefited from the tolerant attitude of Buddhism, which had become the state religion of the whole country by the sixth century. Some practices, such as human sacrifice, were suppressed gradually during the centuries but no attempt was made to outlaw Shamanism and many of its rituals were integrated into Buddhist ceremo-

nies. "Sanshin" the non-Buddhist Mountain God has been deified by Buddhism and his shrine can be found wi-within the walls of most temple complexes. Although Confucianism, more a social ideology code than a religion, was unsympathetic to Shamanism, it failed to supplant it and even adopted some Shamanist elements into its ceremonies such as that dedicated to *Sajik*, the Gods of Land and Harvest. The introduction of Western thought to Korea also had little impact on the practice of Shamanism. On the contrary, the spirit of Shamanism has probably contributed in large measure to the powerful mysticism of Korea's Catholics.

Although in pre-Confucian days, priests or *mudang* came in both sexes, all *mudang* today are women. The job may be handed down from mother to daughter but a true *mudang* is generally chosen by divine inspiration. A girl who shows signs of possession—wild-eyed distraction, singing and proclaiming the gods' presence—will be taken under the wing of a senior Shaman who will teach her the songs and dances of her calling.

A *kut* unfolds with music, dance and song. Offerings are made. Thumping drums set the

Shaman dancing, slowly at first, then fiercely as the gods possess her and speak through her lips. When she is possessed a *mudang* may dance on sharpened blades or press them to her tongue and throat without harm.

Shaman deities live in every room of a Korean house as well as in the world around it. They reside in the gate, the kitchen, atop the storage jars, by the well, even in the toilet. They hover all around and are as much a part of Korean life as rice and *kimch'i*.

Buddhism

Although Buddhism is not the dominant influence in Korean life that it was before the Chosŏn Kingdom reforms in the 14th century, it is still very much alive and well. With some 12 to 15 million lay adherents, Buddhism is Korea's biggest single religion. Of the 18 Buddhist sects two are predominant. The T'aego sect, which permits marriage among its clergy and numbers 2,500 monks and 300 nuns, and the largest, the Chogye sect, which demands celibacy from its 8,000 monks and 5,000 nuns.

Buddhism was, originally, not a religion at all. There was no objet of worship or prayer. It was a doctrine of self-enlightenment, the attainment of which would result in a deep understanding of one's own nature and place in the universe. This in turn would engender a way of being-in-the-world in which suffering would cease to exist and a timeless peace would be enjoyed.

On its long journey from its birthplace in Nepal, however, as it began to appeal to a largely uneducated population, it absorbed a bewildering array of ideas and creeds, saints and saviours, heavens and hells. Some of these were derived

Buddhist ceremony at a temple on Buddha's brithday.

from sound insights into its original esoteric doctrines. Others were mere superstition. In Korea many Shamanistic elements were assimilated.

Buddhism entered Korea in the fourth century through the teachings of Indian, Tibetan and Chinese monks. It spread like wildfire in Paekche and Koguryŏ, quickly becoming the state religion. In Shilla, however, it took some time to gain popularity and it was not until 527 that it became the state religion.

Once Shilla had gained control of the peninsula in 668, establishing a single state, Buddhism as the state religion coexisted peacefully with the increasingly Confucian system of government.

During this period and on into the subsequent Koryŏ Kingdom, Buddhism thrived. Temples became Korea's centres of learning and monks enjoyed privileged roles within

society. Kyŏngju, the capital of Shilla, is today a virtual open-air museum of buddhist relics and art. The Shilla Kingdom, under the leadership of Won'gwang, a monk, developed the *Hwarangdo*, a sort of chivalric order, amongst the youth instilling in them the combined virtues of Buddhism, Taoism and Confucianism—loyalty to the monarch, filial piety, harmony, comradeship, valour in battle, compassion.

As the Shilla and then the Koryŏ Kingdom degenerated so too, spiritually, did Buddhism. Monks became influential courtiers and politicians as worldly and corrupt as the court around them. The corruption and abuses of the monks are reflected in the earthy satire of the village masked dance drama of the time.

The decline in Buddhist influence can clearly be traced to two important moments in Korean history. The first was the 13th century invasion by the Mongols, who set about ravaging the entire country. Taking advantage of the Mongol's fear of the sea the court fled to Kangwhado, an island in the Han-gang River Estuary, where it sought divine assistance by undertaking the immense task of carving the entire bulk of Buddhist scriptures onto wood blocks for printing. This work, the "Tripitaka Koreana", took 16 years to complete and is now on display in the Haein Temple near Taegu. This monumental act, however, failed to defeat the Mongols and naturally, Buddhists were in part blamed for the national disaster. The second movement that influenced the decline of Buddhism was the adoption by Korean scholars of Neo-Confucian doctrines. Early criticism by Neo-Confucian scholars was aimed at the practice, not the institution, of Buddhism, which had become materialistic and worldly later, the Neo-Confucians became antagonistic towards Buddhism itself, holding that its individualistic, other-worldly doctrines would undermine the secular and social values propounded by Neo-Confucianism.

In the mid-14th century,

although actual Mongol occupation of the peninsula was over, Mongol influence at court was still high. Since Buddhists continued to wield great influence at court they were, rightly or wrongly, identified with the pro-Mongol factions. Buddhist power and wealth and the great expense of Buddhist festivals began to be openly criticised by the now influential neo-Confucianists. Thus when General Yi Sŏng-gye staged a revolt and had himself proclaimed king in 1392, he rid the court of both Mongol and Buddhist elements. Although Yi himself and most of the royal and ruling families were Buddhists, the religion had fallen into such disrepute that Yi found it politically expedient to make a complete break with the past.

So began the last Kingdom of Korea, the Chosŏn. Confucianism was the state religion throughout the entire Chosŏn era. Although Buddhism remained the religion of the ruling families it was officially suppressed. Monks were ranked in the lowest social class and even banished from the capital into remote mountain areas. Buddhism became a monastic religion turned in on itself and away from the laymen around it.

The Japanese colonized the country in 1910 and in the interests of strengthening the cultural similarities of the two nations, attempted to amalgamate Japanese and Korean Buddhist sects. These attempts largely failed and may, paradoxically, have revived interest in native Buddhism. Of more lasting harm was the Japanese installation of a variety of sects from Japan that allowed monks to marry and otherwise change Korean Buddhism. This was later the cause of bitter fighting between traditional celibate monks and the newer married orders, and even today, strong differences of doctrine exist in Buddhist Korea.

Buddhism is today enjoying something of a renaissance. In 1975 the Korean government recognized Buddha's birthday as a national holiday, which is joyously celebrated throughout the land. Despite its pacifist doctrines, Korean Buddhism is relatively militant and its adherents fought valiantly against the Japanese colonizers in this century as they did 400 years ago, when warrior monks were organized to fight against Hideyoshi's Japanese invasion. Now, as then, Buddhism plays an active part in the social and political events of the country.

Confucianism

A ritual celebrating Confucius' birthday.

Although Confucian teaching has disappeared as a basis for government and administration, it remains the moral backbone of Korea.

Confucianism was not so much a religion as a social ideology, exacting subordination of the son to the father, of the younger to the elder, of the wife to the husband, of the subject to the throne. It inculcated filial piety, reverence for ancestors and loyalty to friends. Strong emphasis was placed on decorum, rites and ceremony. Scholarship and aesthetic cultivation were regarded as the prerequisites for those in governing or official positions.

While there are records of various forms of Confucian practices throughout Korea's early history, it was not until the 9th century that Confucianism began to gain influence in staunchly Buddhist Korea. In the 10th century, Confucian examinations, called *Kwagŏ*, exactly like those administered in China, were introduced into Korea's bureaucratic qualifications system. Starting in the local primary school, theoretically any male could rise to enter one of the four colleges in the capital and eventually sit the triannual examinations held in the courtyard of Sŏnggyungwan University in Seoul. In practice, only the males of the aristocratic *yangban* class had the time or wealth necessary to study the entire canon of Confucian classics, to write the poetry and practise the calligraphy. Later on, what began as an attempt at model government by an intellectual élite, disintegrated into a system whereby young men with wealthy and powerful families could secure official preferment without actually sitting the examinations.

During much of the Koryŏ Kingdom Buddhism and Confucianism survived side by side. As Buddhism became more and more corrupt this peaceful co-existence began to change and a call for a more moral form of government began to gain great appeal among Korea's intellectuals, especially after the great neo-Confucianist scholar Chu Hsi, entered the court in the 14th century.

In 1392 General Yi Sŏng-gye established the Yi Dynasty and gave official approval to this new stricter variation of Confucian social ethics. Neo-Confucianism froze the social order making filial piety the ultimate social virtue, stressing propriety in social relationships and requiring that ancestor worship be the most important religious ceremony in the household.

At the bottom of this strict social hierarchy were Korean women who receive little or no education and were in virtual bondage throughout their lives, to their fathers, husbands and sons. Women destined to be the wives of *yangban* or aristocrats were educated but the strict code of social behaviour forbade them consorting with unrelated males.

Although Neo-Confucianism had a philosophical foundation, both metaphysical and moral, this aspect was, by and large, not explored in Korea. Koreans tend not to be given to abstract thought, preferring to concentrate on the immediate and practical.

Despite this trend, one philosophical debate of significance did emerge in the Chosŏn dynasty: the so-called ''Four-Seven Debate''. The protagonists in the debate were Yi Hwang, Ki Tae Sung and later scholars. Ancient Chinese sages had declared that there were four features of human nature that were intrinsically good, and seven others that could be good or bad depending on the use made of them. The idea arose that the four were not independently real virtues, but rather given names given to some of the seven, *when they are being rightly used*. The debate between the Korean philosophers was about whether or not the four were

intrinsically good or not.

The interest of the debate from a philosophical point of view lies in a connection with Neo-Confucian metaphysics not noticed by Yi Hwang or Ki Tae Sung. The thesis that the four are not intrinsically good carries the implication that nothing about human nature is intrinsically good. This would seem to be fairly harmless in itself, but in fact it leads to philosophical crisis when combined with the Neo-Confucian metaphysical thesis that reality is a union of two elements, *li* and *ch'i*. *Li* is what gives reality its coherence and shape, and contributes what is intrinsically good in it, while *ch'i* is what *li* shapes into whatever it is, which includes human beings. So, if there is nothing in men that is intrinsically good, we are faced with a dilemma. Either we do not participate in *li* and are utterly different from everything else in the universe, or else *li* is not intrinsically good, in which case there is no intrinsic good in reality at all. Suddenly alienation or nihilism are the deeply *non-Confucian* alternatives available.

Initially Neo-Confucianism was innovative and dynamic. However, Chu Hsi's followers came to regard his philosophy not simply as an ethical way of

life, they saw his work as representing absolute truth. So inflexible was Korea's adherence to confucian doctrine that the Chinese themselves referred to Korea as the ''country of Eastern decorum''. Such fanaticism inevitably led to cultural and intellectual stagnation.

After the deep trauma of Hideyoshi's invasion in the 16th century, reformist Korean scholars began to criticise the bureaucratic corruption and hidebound philosophy of the old order and moved towards a greater awareness of native history and culture. During the two centuries of this Korean Rennaissance the leaders of the *Silhak* (Practical Learning) Movement instigated political and land reforms and encouraged works in the new *hangŭl* alphabet, historical and scientific research and painting, which took on a truly Korean flavour.

Shortly after the last examinations were held at the end of the 19th century Korean Literati lost the political power which they had held for 800 years. When the Japanese usurped power in 1910, the Confucian system disappeared. Its basic values and premises live on in Korea, however, more powerfully than in any other country.

Christianity

One has only to travel a short time in Korea to be amazed at the number of churches one sees. They are everywhere. This alien religion which has failed to gain wide acceptance in China or Japan has taken firm root in Korea. Today there are more than 8 million Christians in Korea, 80 percent of whom are Protestant. While they make up only some 20 percent of the population, they include many leaders of the intellectual and governing élite and so have a disproportionately strong influence on the country's affairs. Unlike many Buddhists, who rarely set foot inside a temple, Korea's Christians are fervent and devout to the point where they would probably feel quite out of place in a Western congregation.

Curiously, the first Christian missionary to arrive in Korea came with the Japanese invasion forces sent by Hideyoshi in 1592. A Spaniard, Gregorio de Cespedes, accompanied the Christian troops which spearheaded the invasion. There is room to speculate that Hideyoshi sent them on this suicidal mission to be rid of them for good. Be that as it may, Cespedes had no influence on Korean beliefs.

Towards the end of the 18th

A Catholic mass at the Myŏng-dong Cathedral in Seoul.

Protestants after a church service.

century Christianity began to trickle into Korea from China and by 1863 there were some 23,000 believers and 12 Korean priests. Although there were sporadic persecutions, on the whole, whether through design or indifference, Catholicism was tolerated. In 1866, however, the young King Kojong was forced by his conservative court to order the public decapitation of Seoul's Bishop and three of his French priests. Persecutions began in earnest and went on unabated until 1876 when Korea was forced to sign treaties with the Western powers guaranteeing the safety and freedom of foreign missionaries.

Christian soldiers, especially Protestant missionaries, began to stream into the country, astutely armed with the modern learning which isolated, withdrawn Korea so badly needed. Their appeal was powerful, the ground ready to welcome them. Buddhism had been tossed aside and isolated in mountain retreats. Shamanism, the spiritual soul of the Han people, was frowned upon as uncouth. Confucianism was stagnant. Apart from ancestor worship and the occasional Shaman kut, there was literally nothing of spiritual substance available to the vast majority of Korean people. The missionaries offered not only spiritual

Taoism and others

enlightenment but also Western learning. They rapidly established schools and colleges for men and women and arranged the advanced education abroad of many of Korea's potential leaders.

American missionaries stood shoulder to shoulder with Koreans during their darkest hours. Throughout the Japanese occupation they gave spiritual support and encouragement to the Korean independence movement until their expulsion en masse in 1940. Christianity in Korea today is synonymous with high moral standards and enlightened learning and has experienced phenomenal growth since the end of the Korean War.

Taoism failed to establish a stronghold in Korea. In its philosophical form its ties with the *Sŏn* sect of Buddhism were too close. In its religious form it too closely resembled Shamanism and was absorbed by it. The only signs of Taoism in Korea now may be found spiritually in a Korean love of nature, harmony and simplicity or practically in the symbols which adorn everyday articles such as the Chinese characters for longevity and happiness. It is most visible on the national flag with its beautiful *Yin-Yang* blue and red symbol representing the dualism of the universe.

Most of Korea's native religions are essentially a mixture of Confucian ethics, Buddhist rites and Taoist beliefs and stem primarily from the *Tonghak* (Eastern Learning) movement which arose in the mid-19th century. Essentially nationalistic and anti-feudal, it preached emancipation and reform. Not basically anti-Catholic, its leaders nevertheless used Catholicism as the whipping post to stir up support amongst the under-privileged. Paradoxically, because its founder, Ch'oe Che-u, claimed to have experienced a vision, believed in one God and used magical symbols, the government lumped him into the same basket as the Catholics and executed him alongside them in 1866. The *Tonghak* and other sects claim some one-and-a-half million devotees in Korea today. They usually venerate a divine leaders or saviour, either living, martyred or legendary and some are ultra-nationalistic, proclaiming Korea as the next world empire.

Taejonggyo followers bow before Tan-gun's portrait.

SUGGESTED FURTHER READING

Buswell, Robert E., Jr. *The Korean Approach to Zen: the Collected Works of Chinul*. Honolulu: University of Hawaii Press, 1983.

Choi Min-hong. *A Modern History of Korean Philosophy*. Seoul: Seong Moon Sa, 1980.

Clark, Charles Allen. *Religions of Old Korea*. Seoul: Royal Asiatic Society, 1961.

Clark. Conald N. *Christianity in Modern Korea*. Washington, D.C.: University Press of America, 1987.

Covell, Alan Carter. *Ecstacy: Shamanism in Korea*. Seoul: Hollym International Corp., 1983.

Huhm, Hala Pai. *Kut: Korean Shamanist Rituals*. Seoul: Hollym International Corp., 1985.

International Cultural Foundation. *Buddhist Culture in Korea* (Korean Culture Series 3). Seoul: Si-sa-yong-o-sa, Inc. 1982.

Kim Yong-choon. *The Ch'ŏndogyo Concept of Man*. Seoul: Pan Korean Book Corp., 1979.

Lee Man-gap. *Ancestor Worship and Korean Society*. California: Stanford University Press, 1983.

Moffet, Samuel H. *The Christians of Korea*. New York: Friendship Press, 1962.

Paik Lak-geon George. *The History of Protestant Missions in Korea, 1832-1910*. Seoul: Yonsei University Press, 1980.

Palmer, Spencer J. *Confucian Rituals in Korea*. Seoul: Po Chin Chai Co., Ltd. 1984.

____. *Korea and Christianity: The Problem of Identification and Tradition*. Seoul: Royal Asiatic Society. 1967.

LANGUAGE AND LITERATURE

Language

Any intelligent foreigner can learn to read and write the Korean script in a matter of hours. Learning to read Korean is infinitely easier than Chinese or Japanese, which require years of painstaking study.

Learning to use the language itself, on the other hand, is much more difficult. Korean is a complex language with a structure very different from Western languages, and so a Gestalt leap in thinking is required to master it. Verbs, especially, are highly developed. With a simple particle inserted into the main verb structure it is possible to express tenses and all manner of moods: suggesting, supposing, wishing, respecting, requesting and more. In its socio-cultural aspect, the language reflects a rigidly hierarchical social struc-ture. You must choose your words carefully depending upon whether you are addressing a child, your boss, a relative or a colleague. In preference to ac-tual names, titles are often used in everyday life. For example, an elderly waitress would be addressed as ''aunt'', and an older person in general conver-sation would be addressed as ''teacher''.

The origins of Korean are obscure. Philologists have yet to solve the puzzle which almost certainly links Korean with the Tungusic languages to its north and with Japanese to its south and east. What is cer-tain is that the Korean language is predominantly that of the Shilla Kingdom which dominat-ed Korea during the seventh century. Unfortunately there is a shortage of documentary evi-dence on the early history of the language due largely to the fact that although Koreans have always been sensitive to the beauty of their language, until relatively recent times what was actually thought to be worth writing down and preserving was predominantly in Chinese.

Korean and Chinese are com-pletely different from one another, both in sound pattern, word formation and sentence structure. Chinese script is often referred to as ideograph-ic, and was originally created from pictures of objects. Koreans could not understand the meaning of texts written in such characters, especially their allusions and metaphors. Shilla Kingdom scholars first deve-loped a system of Chinese characters borrowed in their Chinese meaning but read as a Korean word. This system called *idu* was entirely inade-

A portrait of King Sejong (r. 1418-50) the fourth King of the Chosŏn Period.

quate for proper communication and was largely used to record vernacular songs and poems.

A great breakthrough in communication occurred in 1446 with the development of *hangŭl*, a native Korean script which is alphabetic in character. At the time it was thought important to increase the knowledge of the general populace in medical and agricultural matters, and to this end King Sejong ordered his most respected scholars to develop a script which would enable universal literacy to be attained. Over the years, *hangŭl* has earned great respect internationally for the rationality of its theoretical foundation.

The vocabulary of the modern Korean language is made up of about 40% indigenous words and 60% loanwords, the vast majority of words, which are Chinese. One result is a dual system of native and Sino-Korean numerals. Another is that more formal or academic texts are written in mixed script, with Chinese characters or *hanja* being used for the Chinese loan-words, and *hangŭl* for the purely Korean items. So to read a daily newspaper in Korea you must know at least 1,000 *hanja* and college students need to learn at least twice as many. It is becoming increasingly common, though, to write the lesser-used Sinographs in the native script— even those which are on the Government's list of 1800 Basic Characters. As more and more Chinese words are expressed in *hangŭl*, however, their orgins and even their deeper meanings may become obscured. The communist régime in the north nevertheless abolished the use of *Hanja* shortly after the close of World War II—though for purely nationalistic reasons. In the Republic, however, for the past 40 years, the advantages or disadvantages of the disappearance of Chinese characters from the written language has been the subject of a simmering scholarly dispute between pro-*hangŭl* modernists and those who wish to retain the keys to the language's roots.

Literature

Literature Before Hangŭl (8th to 15th Century)

Early Korean literature consists largely of lyrics for songs and stories of legends and myths. Lacking a native script these early works were transmitted in Chinese. The northern part of the peninsula seems to have developed an epic style appropriate to its harsh climate while a lyric style flourished in the more temperate south.

After the Shilla Kingdom unified the peninsula in the 7th Century Shilla scholars, less influenced by China than its vanquished neighbours, invented a phonetic system using Chinese characters to transcribe Korean sounds. This system called *idu* was used to compose *Hyangga*, entirely national songs native to Korea, of which some 25 have survived.

During the Koryŏ and early Chosŏn Kingdoms vernacular folk literature was abundant but the influence of scholars of classical Chinese was so strong that very little was considered worth preserving.

An alphabet for the Korean language called hunminchŏng-ŭm or "script for the people", in a monument celebrating its creation.

Literature After Hangŭl (15th to 19th Century)

Following the development of *hangŭl* in 1443 increasing numbers of folk songs and poems were recorded in Korean script. To test the new writing system, the king ordered the writing of the *Yong-bi-ŏch'ŏn-ga* (Songs of Flying Dragons), a mighty work celebrating the founding of the Chosŏn Kingdom, comprising some 248 poems. Not only is it the first document ever produced in *hangŭl* it is also an important historical statement of the policies of the Yi Dynasty and a manifesto of their Confucian principles. Comprising heroic tales, foundation myths, folk beliefs and prophecies, it marks the birth of a national vernacular literature. Since verse composition in Chinese was still a qualification for political office, however, widespread use of a vernacular literary form had to await the birth of the reformist movement over two centuries later.

In keeping with the nationalist feeling of the time, enlightened 18th century scholars began creating their own native songs. These were usually in the form of the *sijo*, three lines of about 15 syllables to the line, developed at the end of the Koryŏ Kingdom. Early *sijo* dealt with love, morality and political satire, but later, wittier and more earthy themes were introduced telling tales of domestic disasters and that perennial and universal, favourite, the mother-in-law.

Love stories and tales of valour began to appear in novel form in the 17th century. By the 18th century increasing numbers of satirical and romantic novels appeared culminating in the most famous of Korean novels, 'The Tale of Ch'unhyang'. In this Korean Cinderella story, the young heroine, Ch'unhyang, the illegitimate daughter of a *kisaeng* and the young hero, son of a *yangban* provincial governor fall in love. The inevitable separation ensues. The governor and his son go off to Seoul leaving the poor heroine in the evil clutches of the new governor who attempts to make her his mistress. By law the daughter of a *kisaeng* must herself become one and when she resists she is thrown into prison. The hero eventually returns, exposes the cruel and corrupt governor and marries Ch'unhyang.

This novel and other epic stories were transformed into a sort of wandering minstrel's opera called *p'ansori*, containing narrative and song, a popular theatrical form today. The novel, unfortunately, failed to develop fully. Korea lacked a middle class to support the publication of fiction, the peasantry was largely illiterate and the Confucian establishment esteemed only poetry.

Modern Literature

Literature from around 1900 onwards must be seen in the context of Korea's modern history of foreign domination and national disaster. The Japanese annexation of 1910 and the introduction of Western literary styles resulted in the growth of the *Shinmunhak* or 'New Literary Movement' whose ideas continue to dominate literature in Korea down to the present day.

This movement sought to take literature out of the court and down into the street. The primordial role of literature in their view was to enlighten, educate and liberate. To reach the common man, they integrated the spoken and written languages thereby making their works intelligible to general readers. Poems, short stories, and essays began to appear dealing with nationalistic themes and reflecting the authors' political and social concerns. Censorship by the Japanese government, however, resulted in many authors being imprisoned or executed and for a while the use of the Korean language was prohibited.

In 1912, Yi Kwang Su, the father of modern Korean literature, began to publish his first experimental fiction. Moving completely away from the past he adopted Western writing styles, advocating free love, personal freedom and other revolutionary ideas. A prolific and influential writer, he fell into disrepute when he collaborated with the Japanese colonialists.

Authors of the *Shinmunhak* dealt with both contemporary and historical themes. In Korea the historical novel is not what it is in the West. In the face of cultural genocide, historical novels aimed to remind readers of their national past, their lost independence and reinforce their cultural identity. Lacking publishing houses, these novels were published in the daily newspapers in serialised form, as they continue to be even today. Lofty though their aim was, continual pandering to popular taste made the historical novel over sentimental and melodramatic, crudely portraying scenes of seduction, adultery and cruelty. These and contemporary themes dealing with social injustice and sexual exploitation are extremely popular both in newspapers and on television, unfortunately at the expense of artistic discrimination. The "novel" in Korea is almost synonymous with the newspaper serial and therefore with a lack of artistic integrity.

Writers who wish to see their work critically acclaimed or even published must either write poetry or short stories. To understand the importance of the short story in Korea it is necessary to understand the Korean literary market. An aspiring author in the West would send his book to a publisher and risk either rejection or acceptance. This is not the case in Korea where no publisher would be daring enough to publish a long story by an obscure author. The task of discovering promising writers is in the hands of highbrow literary magazines and because space is limited the short story or poem is preferred.

Modern literature and poetry in Korea is predominantly sombre following the tragic division of the country after the Korean War. Fiction deals with alienation, frustration, the dehumanizing effects of modernization and industrialization. The poetry is nationalistic, melancholic, filled with the emotion the Koreans call *han*—living with loss. Since the late 1960's

A famous novelist Yi Mun-yol (top), Works of prominent Korean novelists (Choi In-hoon, Park Kyong-ni and Kim Song-dong) are now being translated into other languages.

there has been increasing experimentation with modernizing the traditional forms such as the *sijo* and the *p'ansori*.

SUGGESTED FURTHER READING

Language

Baek Eung-jin, *Modern Korean Syntax* Seoul: Jung Min Publishing Co., 1984.

Grant, Bruce K. *A Guide to Korean Characters*. Seoul: Hollym International Corp., 1986.

Huh Woong, *et al. The Korean Language*. Seoul: Si-sa-yong-o-sa, Inc. 1983.

Lee Chung-min. *Abstract Syntax and Korean with Reference to English*. Seoul: Pan Korea Book Corp. 1982.

Lee Hong-bae. *A Study of Korean Syntax*. Seoul: Pan Korea Book

Corp., 1970.

Lee Ki-moon *A Historical Study of the Korean Writing Systems*. English synopsis of the author's *Kugŏ p'yogipŏp ŭi yŏksajŏk yŏngu*. Seoul: Han'guk Yŏnguwŏn, 1963.

____. *Geschichte der Koreanischen Sprache*. Translated by Bruno Lewin. Wiesbaden: Dr. Ludwig Reichert Verlag. 1977.

Park Chang-hai and Park Ki-dawk. *Korean I: An Intensive Course*. Seoul: Yonsei University Press, 1984.

Park Ki-dawk. *Korean 2: An Intensive Course*. Seoul: Yonsei University Press, 1984.

Park Kyu-soh. *The Methodological Theory and Practice of Korean-English Translation*. Seoul: Hanshin Publishing Co., 1986.

Ramstedt, G.J. *A Korean Grammar*. Facsimile reprint, Oosterhout, Netherlands: Anthropological Publications, 1968. Helsinki: Suomalais-ugrilainen Seura, 1939.

____. *Studies in Korean Etymology*. 2 vols. Helsinki: Suomalais-ugrilainen Seura, 1949-1953.

Rucci, Richard B. *Korean with Chinese Characters*, 2 vols, Seoul: Seoul Int'l Publishing House, 1982.

Sohn Ho-min, ed. *The Korean Language: Its Structure and Social Projection*. Honolulu: Center for Korean Studies, Univ. of Hawaii, 1975.

Yi Jong-ho, *Hun-Min-Jeong-Eum (Explanation and Translation of the Right Sound for the Education of the People)*. Seoul: Po Chin Chai, Co., Ltd., 1985.

Literature

Chung Chong-hwa. *Love in Mid-Winter Night: Korean Sijo Poetry*. London: Routledge & Kegan Paul Plc, 1987.

Chung Han-mo, *et al. Mainstreams of Contemporary Poetry*. Seoul: The Korean Culture and Arts Foundation, 1978.

Hong Myoung-hee. *Korean Short Stories*. Seoul: Il Ji Sa Publishing Co., 1975.

Hoyt, James. *Songs of Dragons Flying to Heaven: A Korean Epic*. Seoul: Royal Asiatic Society, 1979.

Hyon Joon-shik. *Modern Korean Short Stories*. New York: Larchwood Publication, 1981.

Kim Dong-uk. *History of Korean Literature*. Translated by Leon Hurvitz. Tokyo: Center for the Study of East Asian Culture, Toyo Bunko, 1980.

Kim Gi-dong. *The Classical Novels of Korea*. Seoul: The Korean Culture and Arts Foundation, 1981.

Kim Jaihium. *Classical Korean Poetry*. Seoul: Hanshin Publishing Co., 1987.

____. *The Contemporary Korean poets*. New York: Larchwood Publication, 1980.

____. *Master Poems From Modern Korea* Seoul:' Seoul: Si-sa-yong-o-sa, Inc. 1980.

____. *Master Sijo Poems From Korea*. Seoul: Seoul: Si-sa-yong-o-sa, Inc. 1982.

Kim Jong-woo. *Postwar Korean Short Stories: An Anthology*. Seoul: Seoul National University Press, 1974.

Kim Yeol-gyu, *et al. The Classical Poetry of Korea*. Seoul: The Korean Culture and Arts Foundation, 1981.

____. *Korean Folk Tales*. Seoul: Si-sa-yong-o-sa, Inc. 1987.

Lee, Grant S. *Life and Thoughts of Yi Kwang-su*. Seoul: U Shin Sa., 1984.

Lee, Peter H. *Anthology of Korean Literature From Early Times to the Nineteenth Century*. Hawaii: University of Hawaii Press, 1981.

____. *Korean Literature: Topics and Themes*. Tucson: University of Arizona Press, 1965.

McCann, David. R. *Black Crane: An Anthology of Korean Literature I & II*. Ithaca: East Asian Papers nos. 14 & 24, Cornell University Press, 1977 & 1980.

O'Rourke, Kevin. *The Cutting Edge: A Selection of of Korean Poetry, Ancient and Modern*. Seoul: Yonsei University Press, 1982.

Rutt, Richard and Kim Chong-un. *Virtuous Women: Three Classic Korean Novels*. Seoul: Royal Asiatic Society, 1974.

Sim Chai-hong. *Fragrance of Spring: The Story of choon Hyang*. Seoul: Po Chin Chai Co., Ltd. 1970.

Skillend, W.E. Kodae Sosŏl: *A survey of Traditional Korean Style Popular Novels*. London: School of Oriental and African Studies, University of London, 1968.

Zong In-sob. *Folk Tales From Korea*. Seoul: Hollym International Corp., 1986.

____. *A Guide to Korean Literature*. Seoul: Hollym International Corp., 1982.

FINE ART

Sŏkkuram Stone Grotto located on Mt. T'ohamsan in Kyŏngju, mid-8th century.

The study and appreciation of Korean fine art has often been neglected, scholars and connoisseurs preferring to concentrate on the more well-known arts of China and Japan. This situation has arisen, in part, due to the latter two countries' greater contact with the West and Korea's relative isolation.

To the casual observer, there is little to distinguish Korea's art from that of its neighbours. However, to one who is prepared to make the effort to learn to appreciate oriental art, Korean art possesses qualities which distinguish it from that of China and Japan and which make it valuable in itself.

The distinctive features of Korean art cannot be described in general terms. A vast array of styles exist in all of the countries of East Asia, and there is considerable overlap. The difference lies in the way Korean fine artists have developed their own way of interpreting and implementing some of the styles which lie within the general mould.

For example, traditional landscape painting in the literati style is common to both Korea and China, yet the particular works painted within that style have different qualities. The Korean landscapes have none of the vast spaces and majesty which characterise many Chinese works. Korea is a smaller country and its mountains have a rounded, green appearance, so its landscape painting tends to be smaller in scope and has a more intimate quality.

The patient and studious scholar of Korean fine art will be able to discover a variety of such differences in "styles within styles".

Painting

Traditional

Despite obvious Chinese influence, early Korean painting has an earthy quality native to the peninsula. Fourth century tomb murals of Shaman deities, dancing and hunting scenes and contemporary customs have great vigour and rhythm. Mountains and animals, flying clouds, flowers, and trees were popular themes. Some of the earliest landscapes known were painted onto wall tiles in the 7th century. Painters from this period were active in Japan and played an important part in the development of Japanese art.

With Buddhism at its height during the Shilla Kingdom (9th century) realistic and spiritual scenes from the Buddhist Sutras were painted. In the Koryŏ Kingdom (10th to 14th century) painting was also the pleasurable pastime of the upper classes. Not only professionals but priests, aristocrats and scholars produced religious paintings, landscapes and portraits, as well as ink pictures of birds, flowers and bamboo.

During the strictly Confucian Chosŏn Kingdom traditional Chinese painting assumed great importance. Korean artists copied the styles of the Sung,

"Kŭmgang Mountain" by Chŏng Sŏn (1676-1759), Ink and watercolour on paper, 128 × 94.5cm, Ho-Am Art Museum.

Yuan and Ming Dynasties of China although a number of paintings of Korean mountain scenes and native flowers and birds did appear.

The 18th century marks a new departure in Korean art. Firstly, Chŏng Sŏn and his followers adapted the techniques of the Chinese Southern School to produce landscapes; secondly, Western methods were introduced to Korea from China; and last, but most decidedly not least, this period marks the growth of the uniquely Korean folk painting.

In Confucian Korea everything outside the élite categories of calligraphy and scholarly or Buddhist painting was classified as folk. These paintings were executed not by unskilled amateurs but by skilled painters who drew their themes from all the religious elements of the country as well as the lives of the common people and the upper classes. They were painted by wandering craftsmen, painter-monks and court artists for display in or on the walls of the royal court, Buddhist temples, Shaman shrines, *Kisaeng* houses and private homes. From the tiger who keeps away the evil spirits, to the humourous scenes of village life, and to the risqué paintings of ladies of doubtful virtue, these delightful works cannot fail to charm anyone who sees them with their freshness and vitality.

A Buddhist painting of the non-Buddhist Mountain God, Sashindo.

Contemporary

In the twentieth century Korean artists began to experiment with Western media, while borrowing certain oriental styles from Japan and continuing to develop the various styles of traditional Korean painting.

Korean artists went to Europe, especially France, to study Western painting and returned to disseminate the techniques of watercolour, oil and acrylic painting. They experimented with the most recent, as well as traditional, styles: abstract expressionism, geometric abstraction, cubism and impressionism. Not always successful in the beginning, Korean attempts to paint in western styles are now beginning to bear fruit, though often without true creativity.

From Japan, Korean artists borrowed a realistic and elaborate style which uses oriental watercolours. Called in Korea *che sek hwa*, this style uses only colour, not the traditional ink and colour, and aims at a realistic representation of the form and colours of the subject.

Munyŏdo by Kim Ki-chang (1913–)

Within Korean painting itself, distinctively Korean styles have emerged but most of these are, unfortunately, lacking in character and creativity. Traditional landscapes and flower-bird paintings are sadly uniform and have none of the subtlety and delicacy of works of earlier periods. However, Buddhist ink painting still displays spontaneity, strength and vigour, while Buddhist paintings of the more elaborate style still exhibit a serenity and solidity of purpose. Folk paintings, also, continue to have quality.

These are, of course, general remarks. It is still possible to find traditional landscape and flower-bird paintings of quality. The works of Kim Ki Ch'ang, Lee Sang Bŏm and Pyon Kwan Sik are refreshing exceptions to the rule.

SH87006 by Kim Tschang-yeul (1929–)

"The More, The Better" a work of the world-famous video artist Paik Nam-jun,
exhibited in the National Museum of Contemporary Art.

Autumn at Samsŏnam Rock on Mt. Kŭmgangsan 1955, by Pyon Kwan-shik (1899-1976)

The White Bull by Yi Chung-sŏp (1916-1956)

Windwave '84 by Ahn Byung-suk (1946–)

Sculpture

Traditional

Early sculpture in Korea is synonymous with the image of Buddha. As Buddhism swept out of India and all over Central and Eastern Asia, images of Buddha in his many incarnations as well as Buddhist saints and minor deities were created in cave sculptures, free standing images and in temples. In Korea Buddhist art reached breathtaking heights during the Shilla Kingdom with the magnificent granite figures in the Sŏkkuram Grotto near Kyŏngju.

The tendency to group all oriental Buddhist sculpture together should be resisted, as in fact each Asian country developed its own quite different style of sculpture, using quite different materials. In China most Buddhas were carved from sandstone or limestone, in Korea from granite and in

Tabot'ap Pagoda in the grounds of Pulguksa Temple in Kyŏngju, Unified Shilla Period

Bronze Bell dedicated to King Sŏngdŏk Unified Shilla, A.D. 771.

Monster's face, a tile of the Paekche Kingdom (18 B.C.-660 A.D.).

Rock-Cut Buddha Triad, 7th century, Paekche: Ht. 2.8m.

Japan from wood, reflecting the materials which were plentiful in each country.

Korea's earliest bronze statuettes are relatively flat and linear, inspired by Chinese calligraphic lines. Perhaps due to the fact that 70% of the country is mountainous, Korean sculptors later developed a love for stone and an enormous skill in working granite. In the 7th century Chinese Buddhas were naturalistic and three dimensional, but by the 8th century they had become excessively fat-faced, even jowled. So prosperous in fact that they lost their spiritual aura. Korean Buddhas on the other hand had, by the 8th century, become highly spiritual, with graceful faces, long straight noses, flowing lines. The giant free-standing image at Sŏkkuram is the quintessence of Buddhism's spiritual momentum in the Far East.

So sublime was Buddhist art in Korea at its height that it was eagerly copied and absorbed by the Japanese. Koreans who went to Japan were overwhelmed with honours so that they would stay to build Japan's buildings, sculpt her statues and cast her bells. Korea's beautiful and melodious bronze bells are not mere temple paraphernalia, but major works of sculpture inspired by a fervent devotion to Buddha and playing a major role in ritual and worship.

Excellent images continued to be made in the Koryŏ Kingdom but the quality and quantity of Buddhist sculpture declined along with Buddhism itself during the Chosŏn Kingdom.

Contemporary

After the Japanese occupation in 1910 Japan became the window onto the world for Koreans. Young Koreans travelled to Japan to study the unfamiliar world of European art. They returned armed with the spears of academic realism which reigned supreme in Japanese art circles. Despite the zeal of these young pioneers, sculpture lacked creative inspiration.

Following the Korean War artists experimented with various Western styles and fashions. By the late 1950's sculptors had divided into schools of realism and abstractionism and were employing a greater diversity of materials, but by the 1970's young artists had moved almost completely towards pure abstractionism. Sculpture in the Eighties is richer and more diversified with artists seeking a warmer, more humane style in reaction to the stark intellectualism of the previous decade.

Calligraphy

In Korea, as in China and Japan, calligraphy is an art form to be displayed and admired like a painting. In fact, painting and calligraphy are twin arts in the Orient. The same brush and ink are used, and paintings are prized for the strength, vitality and spontaneity of the calligraphic lines used to depict the subject matter.

In old Korea calligraphy was not only a means of communication but a mental discipline for the cultured classes, and full of philosophical implications. Like the Chinese masters, Korean calligraphers felt that every stroke and dot should suggest a natural object infused with life.

Few examples of Korean calligraphy survived the Japanese invasions in the 16th century. Those stone monuments and

tablets which did survive show a vigorous angular style in the 5th century, for instance, as befits the military state which ruled the north, or later, a more regular squarish style during the Shilla and Koryŏ Kingdoms.

When calligraphy became a prerequisite for official position during the Chosŏn Kingdom, there was an upsurge of interest amongst the upper classes, who became skilled at mastering the prevailing Chinese techniques.

Not until the 18th century with its greater interest in all things Korean did calligraphers adopt a dynamic style of their own. With the Japanese domination of the country in the early 20th century, calligraphy became Japanized and after World War II survived only as a minor art. Since 1960, however, there has been renewed interest in calligraphy including experimentation with the Korean alphabet.

The National Museum of Contemporary Art located in Kwach'ŏn, in the southern suburbs of Seoul.

SUGGESTED FURTHER READING

Choi Sun-u. *5000 Years of Korean Art*. Seoul: Hyonam Publishing Co., 1979.

Covell, Alan Carter. *Folk Art and Magic*. Seoul: Hollym International Corp., 1985.

Covell, Jon Carter. *Korea's Colorful Heritage*. Seoul: Seoul: Si-sa-yong-o-sa, Inc. 1987.

____. *The World of Korean Ceramics*. Seoul: Seoul: Si-sa-yong-o-sa, Inc. 1987.

The Flavor of Korean Painting. Seoul: Korea Britannica, 1972.

Honey, William B. *Korean Pottery*. London: Faber and Faber, 1947.

Kim Che-won and G. St. Gompertz, G.M. *The Ceramic Art of Korea*. London: Faber and Faber, 1961.

Kim Che-won and Kim Won-yong. *The Arts of Korea*. London: Charles E. Tuttle Co., 1966.

Kim Che-won and Lena Kim Lee. *Arts of Korea*. Tokyo: Kodansha International, 1974.

Kim Dong-uk. *et al. Korean Culture and Arts*. Seoul: The Korean Culture and Arts Foundation, 1981.

Kim Won-yong. *Art and Archaeology of Ancient Korea*. Seoul: Taekwang Publishing Co., 1986.

____. *Korean Art Treasure*. Seoul: Yekyong Publications Co., Ltd. 1986.

Korea National Commission for UNESCO. *Traditional Korean Art*. Seoul: Seoul: Si-sa-yong-o-sa, Inc. 1983.

____. *Traditional Korean Painting*. Seoul: Seoul: Si-sa-yong-o-sa, Inc. 1983.

McCune, Evelyn B. *The Art of Korea, An Illustrated History*. Rutland, Vt., and Tokyo: Charles E. Tuttle Co., Inc., 1962.

____. *The Inner Art*. Seoul: Po Chin Chai Co., Ltd., 1983.

Swann, Peter. *Art of China, Korea, and Japan*. London: Thames and Hudson, revised, 1967.

PERFORMING ARTS

Probably one of the richest aspects of Korean culture is its legacy of music and dance. On the whole, solo music yields pride of place to ensemble performance and generally speaking, dance is an essential component of much traditional musical performance, whether it be ritualistic temple dance, the slow, measured dances of the court or the lively uninhibited folk dances of the people.

To the Western ear schooled in the seven-note scale, traditional Korean music with its five-note scale often sounds "out of tune." This seeming lack of harmony is made up for by its dramatic shifts in rhythm and metre, its sudden pauses and its subtle undertones.

Legend has it that over a thousand years ago a great Shilla king sat in the moonlight gazing out to sea. So moved was he by the beauty of the night he began to play a haunting melody on his jade flute. As he played the waves of the sea grew still and calm. The haunting music of the lives on in the bamboo *taegŭm* and is the very melody of Korea's woods and mountains. The *taegŭm*, the *changgo* or hourglass drum, the beautiful 6 or 12 string zither and the bells, gongs and stone chimes are now the most popular of Korea's many traditional musical instruments.

Koreans love to sing. The popular music of the older generation is either the gutsy Korean folk song or the *ppongtchak norae* songs, reminiscent of Japanese popular songs of twenty or thirty years ago. The younger generation enjoy songs based on contemporary. Western ballads and rock music. Of enormous appeal to young and old alike is Western classical music, and in recent years Korean performers have gained critical acclaim both here and abroad.

Koreans also love to dance, and the mood and atmosphere created by the dancer are all important. The Korean court dancer spent years learning the rigorous techniques and movements of the dances, yet such study was only a prelude to the real dance. It provided the tools which could be used to transcend techniques and prescribed steps, and create unique movements, moods and atmosphere.

Music

Traditional

Korean traditional music is predominantly that of the Chosŏn Kingdom (1392-1910). Music from earlier times received its final formulation in that period and recent music written in traditional style takes its models from that era. Music reflects the basic division of Korean society during those five centuries between the upper and the lower classes. The aristocratic *Chŏng-ak* music, stately, solemn, ritualistic, comprises Confucian ceremonial music and the music of the Confucianist court. The commoners *Sog-ak*, lively, lusty, vibrant, includes Shaman and Buddhist music, folk and farmers' music, narrative opera and instrumental solo music.

During the 15th century, King Sejong, famous for his cultural contributions to Korea, began the systematic recording of *Chŏng-ak* music. During his reign and that of his successors, music and dance were classified and recorded and performances and costumes were standardized. Thanks to these enlightened Chosŏn kings, ancient Chinese music and dance long since lost to the Chinese themselves, can be enjoyed in its authentic form only in Korea. Twice a year Confucian music and dance is performed at Sŏnggyun-gwan University in Seoul and every May the ancestor rite is performed at the Chongmyo Royal Shrine.

All forms of court music continue to be performed on the Korean stage. These forms include native Korean music written for court banquets (*hyang-ak*), military music (*ch'wit'a*), Korean chamber music (*p'ungnyu*), lyric songs (*kagok*) and the indigenous Korean sonnet, the *sijo*, set to music.

Where the court music is slow and sedate, by contrast the *Sog-ak* music of the common folk is energetic and emotional. It is this music and its accompanying dance which is most accessible to the foreigner. Folk music can include not only the work songs and lullabies of the labourer and the housewife but also the more polished songs of the itinerant entertainers. Like their mediaeval European counterparts, these bands of troubadours, acrobats, story tellers, musi-

P'iri and Kŏmun-go, traditional Korean musical instruments.

Chŏng-ak, a performance of court music performance.

clans, and mendicant priests carried music and song throughout Korea for centuries. Modern media and Korean's penchant for Western music have marked their demise. They live on only in the ''farmers bands'' which perform at festivals.

One of the great solo forms of folk music which seems to be regaining popularity with the young generation is the narrative opera or *p'ansori*. Developed out of the folk singing style of the Southwest, the stories are based on popular tales similar to those in the West, the devoted daughter story, the good and evil brothers, the Cinderella story, tales of valour and tales of humour. The solo *p'ansori* singer is always accompanied by barrel drum and he or she sings all the roles and recites the narrative between the songs. In the past a complete *p'ansori* could last up to six hours. Performances these days usually last about two and a half hours and only a segment of the story is presented at the sitting.

Contemporary

Western music is believed to have been introduced into Korea by the foreign missionaries just before the turn of the century through the teaching of psalms and hymns. It has flourished enormously in Korea since then—especially since the end of the Korean War. The quality of Korean composition and performance showed a marked improvement with the return in the Sixties of numbers of musicians from studies abroad.

By far the form of classical music with the broadest appeal in Korea is the opera, whether foreign or foreign-inspired. Seoul now boasts as many as three or four concerts a night, performed by Korea's excellent symphony orchestras, chamber music ensembles, opera companies and choirs. Many young Korean musicians now figure prominently on the classicial music scene including one of the world's greatest violinists, Chung Kyung-Wha, and her international prize-winning brother, the pianist Chung Myung-Whun worked as the conductor of the Bastille Opera in Paris.

On October 8, 1995, the KBS (Korea Broadcasting System) Symphony Orchestra gave a special concert under the baton of pianist-conductor Chung Myung-Whun at the United Nations General Assembly Hall in New York to celebrate the 50th anniversary of the world body's founding as well the 50th anniversary of Korea's Liberation.

About 1,800 people packed the Hall, led by U.N. Secretary-General Boutros Boutros-Ghali and including ambassadors and diplomats assigned to the United Nations as well as U.N. personnel, and representatives of the U.N.

peace keeping forces.

The programme included Beethoven's triple concerto by Chung, his sister Chung Myung-Wha (cello) and Kim Young-Uck (violin), the Mad Scene aria of Donizetti's Opera, Lucia di Lammermoor, sung by Soprano Shin Young-Ok, and Concerto for Samul-Nori (Korean percussion music) by Kim Duk-Soo's team.

Such Korean musicians as Jo Su-Mi (soprano), Hong Hei-Kyung (soprano), Jennifer Koh (violinist), Sarah Chang (violinist), Han Na Chang (cellist) are world-renowned.

Dance

Traditional

One of the most distinctive aspects of Asian culture is its tradition of dance with its deep religious element, embellished and altered through the centuries, beloved and practised by its people. What in the West is a secular and peripheral amusement, an entertaining way to spend an evening, is to Asians absolutely central to their culture. Nowhere is this truer than in Korea with its vast repertory of religious, court and folk dancing.

Unlike Western classical dance, Korean dance, in the main, demands no rigorous techniques which must be mastered and respected with every performance. On the contrary, spontaneity and improvization are crucial, with the dancer devising her own personal choreography, not to tell a story, but to create a mood. The two key concepts in Korean dances are *hŭng* (the inner mood) and the *mŏt* (charm, grace, spiritual inspiration), without which a dance is only a series of movements lacking inner fire.

The dancer uses the body as a fluid unit moving the shoul-

ders and upper body, arms floating wide, back erect, one knee raised slightly, with the foot upwards, stepping and turning on the heel. In many women's dances the foot is rarely seen at all being hidden under the floor-length Korean skirt. In certain dances these flowing garments and fluid movements make the dancer appear to float across the stage. One of the most distinctive poses in a Korean dance is the suspended position, balancing on one foot with the free leg extended while the shoulders softly rise and fall. With this movement a great dancer can

convey the deepest sense of ecstatic power. Ecstasy is the very watchword of Korean dance, not only in the shaman and folk dance but even in the formal court dances.

Sacred and magical in origin, dance is permeated with Korea's most ancient belief, Shamanism. During the Shilla Kingdom the famed *hwarang* youths, Korea's knights, entertained the court with ancient songs and dances from Korea's countryside embellishing them with tales from their own time. One of the oldest of the court dances, the *Ch'ŏyong* Dance, originated in this way. As

Buddhism took firm root in Korea during the Koryŏ Kingdom many dances were imported from China for Buddhist rituals, influencing and being influenced by Shamanist ritual dancing as the centuries passed.

During the Chosŏn Kingdom the famed *kisaeng* became preeminent in court dancing. With her regal attire and her distinctive Korean hair pin, she is the unshakeable symbol of Korean grace and beauty, featured on tourist posters throughout the world.

It is thanks to King Sejong (15th century), the fourth ruler of the Chosŏn Kingdom and his cultivated successors that music and dance was codified and recorded enabling ancient dances to be reconstructed and performed to this day.

Korean dance takes three major forms; court, religious and folk. Traditional court dances are of two distinctive types, those of Korean and those of Chinese origin. They have relatively simple steps and elaborate costumes. The most commonly seen dance is the *Hwagwanmu*, the "Flower Crown Dance", named for the sparkling coronet worn by the performers. As in all court dance, the dancers wear long sleeves over their hands which they swirl about adding colour

and excitement to the otherwise slow, graceful movements. With its refined and distinctive style, Korean court dancing was much prized by the Chinese T'ang Emperors and Korean dances were part of the classical repertory of the Chinese Court.

Religious dances also come in three distinct types, Shaman, Buddhist and Confucian. The Shaman dances performed by the female *mudang* are central to the exorcism rite and are used to invoke the spirits and to send the *mudang* into a trance. Buddhist dances are used to smooth the way for departed souls on their journey to heaven. Highly ceremonial Confucian dancing, originating in China but now only seen in Korea, is comprised of dances in honour of Confucius performed twice a year at Sŏnggyungwan University and those performed at the Royal Ancestral Shrine once a year. They are distinguished by stiff movements and reverent bowing and differ mainly in the number of dancers in each.

It is folk dancing which is most quintessentially Korean. Evolved from Shamanistic ceremonies over 3,000 years old, it is in these dances that the idea of expressing inner emotions through outward

Parach'um, or cymbal dance, a Buddhist ritual dance performed by two or four monks.

gestures is most apparent.

The oldest and most popular folk dance is the "Farmer's Dance". Today's version is a mixture of two forms, one fast-paced and acrobatic, the other more refined and intricate. From the first comes the twirling hat with its eccentric streamer, from the second this distinctive big paper-flowered hats which bob with every turn. With an ear-splitting din of gongs and drums, dancers spin and leap about madly as they go from house to house chasing the evil spirits from hearth and home.

The colourful masked dance drama is believed to have come from Central Asia as part of the sweeping trail of Buddhist

A court dance performance.

culture which descended on Korea in the 7th century. Religious in its origins, the beautiful masks were sacred and burned after each performance. In feudal Korea, however, the masked dance dramas became satires portraying the foibles of corrupt monks, lecherous old *yangban*, greedy merchants, scolding housewives and charlatan Shamans. It is the *Pongsan* or "Lion Dance" which is commonly performed today. Originally the lion, unknown in Korea, devoured sinners against Buddha but he now vigorously swallows up the silly aristocrats and the wicked priests. With its mixture of song, dance, pantomime, improvised comic dialogue, colourful costumes and magnificent masks, this is the closest to pure theatre that old Korea ever got.

Of Korea's other folk dances the most powerfully expressive are the *Sŭngmu* and the *Salp'uri*. The *Sŭngmu*, or "Monk's Dance", is said to have evolved from the ancient legend of a beautiful *kisaeng* who was determined to seduce a monk famous for his celibacy. In Buddhist robes and hat, the *kisaeng* went to the monk's cave and slowly began beating a thrilling rhythm on her drum. Faster and faster she went, swaying and dancing before the entranced monk. When, at the end, her robes slipped to the ground, the poor monk was completely overcome and eager for seduction. Performed solo, the dancer appears in hooded monk's garb and dances around a large drum, alternately drawn and repelled. Finally, unable to resist, the dancer draws two sticks from his robe and plays a breathtaking solo on the drum. The speed builds up until the drummer gives up, exhausted. The quality of the Monk's Dance depends entirely on the performer's inner inspiration. Performed by the best this dance can leave its audience in tears. An offshoot of this dance is the sensational "Drum Dance". Performed by glamorously costumed young women, this is considered to be Korea's youngest and liveliest folk dance.

In the *Salp'uri* the dancer's skill is everything as she strives to cleanse her spirit of anguish, sweeping her audience from sad quietude to ecstatic joy in the space of a few minutes. Without true spiritual inspiration it is nothing but a series of movements with a scarf. When performed with powerful emotion it is the epitome of Korean dance.

Contemporary

Contemporary dance arrived in Korea during the Japanese occupation in the early Twenties. In 1922, Baku Ishii, a pioneer of modern dance in Japan and former student of Isadora Duncan, visited Seoul to perform his "Dance Poem". From that moment increasing numbers of students, smitten with this new form, left for Japan to study under the master.

Through the dark years of the occupation and the aftermath of the Korean War, young dancers sought to reconcile classical Western techniques with the themes and emotions of Korean dance. Since the two are basically incompatible this has been a difficult task. Western ballet is physically dynamic, often sexual, dominating space and playing with light and sound. In Korean dance sexuality is suppressed, physical motion is minimal and inner spirituality is all. To add to these problems, the National Ballet Company formed in 1973 at first suffered from a chronic lack of male dancers. While remaining a minor art form, the ballet scene in Korea has, nevertheless, been greatly invigorated since 1984 by the formation of a private company—the Universal Ballet Company—which employs American teachers and often performs with foreign dancers.

Korean dancers have successfully staged American and British musicals. In recent years the government has increasingly encouraged experimental dance troupes striving to create a dance form which will appeal to both audiences at home and abroad.

SUGGESTED FURTHER READING

Heyman, Alan C. *Dances of the Three-Thousand-League Land.* Seoul: Dong-a Publishing Co., 1964.

Kim Chʼŏn-hŭng, Heyman, Alan C. "Korean Traditional Dance." *Korea Journal, Vol. 15 (Feb. 1975), 51-55.*

Kim Yang-kon "Farmers Music and Dance." *Korea Journal*, Vo.. 7 (Oct. 1967), 49.

King, Eleanor, "Reflelctions on Korean Dance." Korea Journal, Vol. 17 (Aug. 1977), 36-55.

Korean National Commission for UNESCO. *Traditional Korean Music.* Seoul: Seoul: Si-sa-yong-o-sa, Inc. 1983.

Lee Hye-ku. *An Introduction to Korean Music and Dance.* Seoul: Royal Asiatic Society, 1977.

____. *Essays on Korean Traditional Music.* Seoul: Seoul Computer Press, 1983.

Pratt, Keith. *Korean Music: Its History and Its performance.* Seoul: Jung Eum Sa, 1987.

Province, Robert C. *Essays on Korean Traditional Music.* Seoul: Royal Asiatic Society, 1980.

Rockwell, Coralie J. *Kayago: The Origin and Evolution of the Korean 12-String Zither.* Seoul: Royal Asiatic Society, 1974.

Song Bang-song, *Source Reading in Korean Music.* Seoul: Korean National Commission or UNESCO, 1980.

Film

After years in the doldrums, Korean film is beginning to make its mark on the international scene. In the Eighties, Korean films have harvested prizes at the various film festivals around the world. Notably Kang Suyŏn who won "Best actress' award at the 1987 Venice Film Festival for her role in "The Surrogate Mother". More importantly, the public is returning to the cinema and this increased commercial success hopefully bodes well for the quality of future Korean films.

Korea's first film, a kinodrama—a play with motion picture inserts—was made in 1919. The first silent movie appeared 4 years later and the first "talkie", Ch'unhyang-jŏn, based on Korea's most popular folk tale, was released in 1935. All in all this story of true love, long suffering virtue and triumph over evil has been filmed about a dozen times so far.

During the war years the films industry was turned into a Japanese propaganda machine. After liberation in 1945 there was a flurry of activity, not noted for its quality, which was cut short by the Korean War. The industry recovered briefly in the mid-Fifties thanks to new equipment supplied under for-

A scene from the movie, Sŏp'yŏnje, which won the awards for Best Director and Best Actress at the 1st Shanghai Int'l Film Festival in 1993 and shattered Korean box office records by drawing over 1 million viewers.

eign aid programmes and the government dropping the entertainment tax on cinema tickets.

For the next two decades Korean cinema was largely stagnant. The public deserted the box office for television and government censorship, direct and indirect, prevented Korean directors from attempting anything remotely controversial or experimental. Box-office successes tended to be "kung-fu" films, melodramatic soap operas, youthful comedies of horseplay and hormones and patriotic historical epics.

In the early Eighties three factors contributed to a renaissance of the cinema industry. Technical standards improved, the government distributed subsidies free from political constraints and the public was bored with low quality television productions.

One of the most successful films of recent years is "Gam-

ja" (potato). Filmed in a style similar to the French "filme d'auteur" where the director's interpretation supersedes the actual story line, it depicts a view of the hopelessness of life in colonial times through the trials and tribulations of its young heroine. Set in Japanese-ruled Korea of the Twenties it tells the story of a young potato-field worker and her indifferent husband, her seduction by a wealthy landowner and her ultimate destitution.

Despite its gloomy theme the director, Byun Chang-ho, has imbued the film with a sort of serious lightness; a complete departure from the tear-jerking melodramas of previous years.

Well-acted and beautifully photographed it remains to be seen whether this is a new door opening onto a world of genuine creativity or whether it will simply spawn a series of lesser films along the same lines.

Drama

In Korea there were no dramatic forms except those that appeared as forms of dance, until the advent of Western type drama around the turn of the century. A relative boom in the Thirties was not sustained. The Confucian upper classes regarded drama as trivial and Korea lacked an urban middle class to support the theatre. Political upheaval in the Fifties and Sixties together with the introduction of motion pictures, consigned modern drama to the backwater where it remains today. Drama is now only performed in small theatres and restaurants to mostly young audiences.

Korea's traditional puppets date from ancient times. There was once a large repertory of these colourful puppet plays but only one, the satirical *Kkoktukakshi* has survived and is performed today.

SUGGESTED FURTHER READING

Amemiya, Chan, "Origins of Korean Mask Dance Drama. "*Korea Journal*, Vol. 17 (Jan. 1977), 57-64.

Choi Sun-u. "The Masks of Korea: The Case of Hahoe Masks." *Korea Jounrnal*, Vol. 19 (Apr. 1979), 45-50.

Kim Dong-uk. "On P'ansori." *Korea Journal*, 13 (Mar. 1973), 10-17.

Korean National Commission for UNESCO. *Korean Dance, Theater and Cinema.* Seoul: Seoul: Si-sa-yong-o-sa, Inc. 1983.

____. *Traditional Performing Arts of Korea.* Seoul: Seoul Computer Press, 1986.

Lee Hyu-ku. "Korean Masque Drama." *Korea Journal* Vol. 1 (Mar. 1961), 25-27.

Rhie Sang-il. "Dramatic Aspect of Shamanistic Rituals." *Korea Journal*, Vol. 15 (Jul. 1975) 23-28.

Yoh Suk-kee. "Traditional Korean Plays and Humor." *Korea Journal, Vol. 10 (May 1970), 19-22.*

Contemporary drama.

CRAFTS

Pottery

Koreans have produced a staggering array of beautiful handicrafts over the centuries. Splendid bronze bells, exquisite gold crowns and jewellery, gold and gilt reliquaries and ornamentation exist in great quantity. But perhaps it is for their magnificent ceramics that Koreans are most famous.

Most celebrated of all are the celadon porcelains produced during the Koryŏ Kingdom. The marvellous blue-green glaze, simple designs and elegant flowing lines of Korean celadon have drawn the admiration of collectors down the ages. The Chinese themselves considered the colours of

Koryŏ celadons so perfect that they declared them to be one of the ten most wonderful things in the world—the other nine being Chinese.

By the mid-12th century, Korean potters had developed their unique inlay method. Designs were inscribed into the wet clay, then the entire piece was smeared with white clay. When the excess white clay was wiped away from the surface, the inlaid designs remained filled with white. The piece was then glazed with celadon and fired.

The techniques of Koryŏ celadon were lost during the Mongol invasions, and although modern potters reproduce the

shapes and inlays of the originals the colours cannot compare.

Chosŏn craftsmen produced luminous white porcelain which was also much admired by the Chinese court. By the mid-Chosŏn period in the 17th and 18th centuries, kilns were producing enormous quantities of this porcelain. Most of them were located along an 80-mile stretch of the Han-gang River, drawing wood from neighbouring forests with disastrous consequences for the local environment.

A cruder, more humble porcelain also existed side by side with the aristocratic whites. Made of the same greyish clay

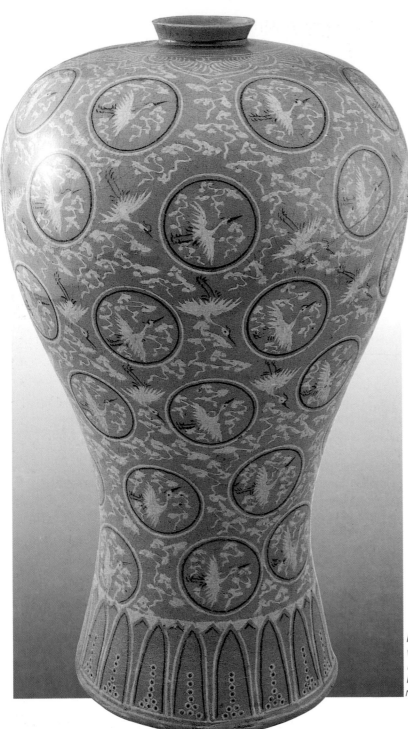

as the Koryŏ celadons, *punch'ŏng* slip was often roughly painted onto the surface and a design was freely inlaid, stamped, painted or even scratched onto the slip. This bold, colourful *punch'ŏng* ware was essentially for use by the commoners but Japanese collectors were later charmed by its artlessness and paid huge sums for *punch'ŏng* tea bowls.

Like so many aspects of Korean cultural life, the invasions by the Japanese in the 16th century marked the downfall of Korean ceramics. The Japanese carried off whole villages of potters to Japan to save themselves the expense of importing ceramic art from China.

Korean pottery is slowly recovering from this and subsequent dissasters such as the Japanese colonization of 1910 and the Korean War and today's ceramics display the same beauty of form and simplicity of design which have been its hallmarks throughout the centuries.

Maebyŏng Vase, porcelain with celadon glaze and inlaid decoration. Koryŏ Dynasty, mid-12th century.

KOREA:

Its History and Culture

Published by
Korean Overseas Information Service
Copyright © 1996
All rights reserved

Text and maps prepared by
Chris Wright, Ph.D (Cantab)

Designed by
Ad Point: Dong Hwa Bldg., 609, 43-1,
1-ga, Pill-dong, Chung-gu, Seoul, Korea

Printed by
Jungmunsa Munhwa Co., Ltd.
Songsandong 208-10, Mapo-gu, Seoul, Korea

ISBN 89-7375-302-9 03910